W9-ANK-386

By The Same Author

PEOPLE WHO MAKE THINGS:
How American Craftsmen Live and Work

AMISH PEOPLE:
Plain Living In A Complex World

(MARGARET K. MC ELDERRY BOOKS)

ESKIMOS
Growing Up
In A Changing Culture

ESKIMOS
Growing Up In A Changing Culture

by CAROLYN MEYER

with research assistance from
BERNADINE LARSEN

photographs by John McDonald

A Margaret K. McElderry Book

ATHENEUM / 1977 / NEW YORK

6/79 Barnett 3/-

J
301.45
M

39590

Library of Congress Cataloging in Publication Data
Meyer, Carolyn.
Eskimos.
"A Margaret K. McElderry book."
SUMMARY: Describes the life of Alaskan Eskimos
and their dilemma in trying to reconcile the white
man's ways with their ancient culture.
1. Eskimos—Alaska—Social conditions—Juvenile
literature. 2. Eskimos—Alaska—Social life and
customs—Juvenile literature. [1. Eskimos—
Alaska—Social life and customs] I. Larsen,
Bernadine. II. McDonald, John.
III. Title.
E99.E7M545   301.45'19'7073   77-9472
ISBN 0-689-50078-5

Copyright © 1977 by Carolyn Meyer
All rights reserved
Library of Congress catalog card number 77–8560
ISBN 0–689–50078–5
Published simultaneously in Canada by
McClelland & Stewart, Ltd.
Manufactured in the United States of America by
The Murray Printing Company
Forge Village, Massachusetts
Designed by Marjorie Zaum
First Edition

For the Real People of Alaska

Contents

Part 1

BREAKUP

CRAMMED IN THE NARROW SEAT NEXT TO THE MAIL SACKS
and freight in the single-engine plane, Jim Koonuk stares
down at the flat, treeless, frozen tundra of southwestern
Alaska. Jim is sixteen years old, a high school junior, and
an Eskimo, and he has cut his classes to go home for seal
hunting. Home is Chaputnuak, a tiny coastal village on the
Yukon-Kuskokwim Delta, a hundred miles from Bethel
and the regional high school that draws students from an
area of one hundred thousand square miles.

For weeks the men of the villages near the Bering Sea
have been taking their snow machines out over the shelf
ice to open water to hunt. But soon the shelf ice will begin
to break off and move out to sea, the men will put their
boats into the water between the ice floes, and the hunting
will begin in earnest, day after long day. It is a dangerous

business, but their food supply depends on it, as it has for thousands of years. Jim cannot bear to miss it.

When he flew this way at Christmas, a vast white emptiness stretched endlessly in all directions. But now the sun is moving north, and the course of the Kuskokwim River sidewinding toward the sea is unmistakable. Creeks and streams are dark threads lacing the river to the lakes and ponds. Dark patches of shrubs and lichens have erupted through the snow.

Soon now—it can happen any time from the end of March to late May—the river ice will groan and shriek as it rends itself apart and starts its annual move down to the sea. All over Alaska people are betting money on the exact minute when the ice of the big rivers—the Yukon and the Tanana and the Kuskokwim—will begin to move.

Breakup is a momentous happening in the far north, one of the turning points of the year. The tundra will change from an unbroken expanse of frozen wasteland, where exposure can mean painful frostbite in seconds and death in minutes, to a spongey marsh where wildlife breeds in profusion and grasses and flowering plants display their splendid colors during the brief, intense growing season. At the other side of the year, freeze-up—the second crucial but more subtle turning point—will transform the tundra back to featureless whiteness again.

"A few more minutes," the pilot shouts over the roar of the engine. "Bethel airport said the visibility out here was three miles."

They both laugh. Weather on the coast changes fast.

A strong south wind has kicked up a ground blizzard, and a veil of whirling snow has dropped visibility to less than a quarter of a mile. The pilot, a white man used to flying in the "bush," as rural Alaska is called, settles his plane lower, and they catch a glimpse of the bright orange windsock at the Chaputnuak airstrip. The plane swoops toward it like a bird after an insect, banking low over the small houses strung out between the river and the pond still hidden beneath the snow. Jim can see a half-dozen snowmobiles racing over the frozen pond toward the landing strip, to fetch the mail, to cart the freight, to bring back any passengers. Breakup, when it comes, will change that. For a few weeks transportation will be a problem, as the tundra shifts from winter to that second season of the arctic year, the quick succession of spring, summer, and fall. Then it will be a world of outboard motorboats and muddy walking, of taking the long way around the pond.

The stall signal howls and the plane bumps down the short, icy strip. By the time the pilot swings around and taxis back to the men with their machines and sleds, Jim has spotted his Uncle Wally, his cousins John and Tony, his friend Dennis. Jim is home again, where he knows he belongs.

The village of Chaputnuak is a fictitious village, but it is also a *real* one—real in the sense that this is what an Eskimo village in southwestern Alaska is like. The Koonuk family—Jim and his parents and brothers and sisters and other relatives, which include in one way or another most of the people of Chaputnuak—is a fictitious family, but it is real in that same sense: this is how many Eskimos of this area live, and how they sometimes feel about themselves and about an outside world that is continually affecting their ancient culture, even when it cannot completely change or absorb it.

April

GRAY MORNING, BARELY DAYLIGHT. THE MEN EASE THEIR boats off the ice-bound beach, into the black water, and start the outboard motors. There are two or three men in each boat. Jim, with his father's brothers, Wally and David, in the last of the eight boats, nervously fingers his powerful .222 rifle. It is the first time he has been allowed to go seal hunting this early in the spring. When he was younger he had gone out with his uncles only after the ice had cleared and most of the danger was past. Then for the past two years he had sat in a classroom in Bethel, miserable and unable to concentrate, thinking of what he was missing back home. And when he had gone out late in May, after school was over, his luck was "bum." The sense of danger and the hope that today he will get his first big seal are exhilarating. But he sits motionless and silent while

Wally maneuvers the skiff among the drifting ice floes.

The seals, like the hunters, have been waiting for breakup. All winter they stayed under the ice, feeding on the few fish available, coming up regularly to their breathing holes. Soon they will wriggle up on land to bear their pups and to breed again, but now they swim freely in the leads—pronounced LEEDS, the channels between the ice floes—their streamlined heads breaking the surface of the dark water, disappearing instantly at the slightest sound. Wally has cut the motor; they paddle silently among the floes. In the far distance they hear the faint crack of a rifle shot. No one speaks. They study the water, push away floating pieces of ice that might clunk against the boat. Jim's gaze wanders and then halts suddenly. He gestures to David, trying to conceal his excitement. David nods and waits for the seal to come closer. If he shoots at this distance the seal, thin from a long winter of poor eating, may sink before they can get to it.

Although he itches to try, Jim knows that he must not shoot. That right belongs to only one man at a time in each boat—to do otherwise would be dangerous—and it was agreed that David would be first. The seal disappears suddenly; when it comes up again it is farther away, not closer. David curses softly and lowers his rifle.

The morning passes. They hear more shots from the other boats, and they spot several more seals, only one close enough to shoot. But it is not close enough to reach, and by the time they get there it has sunk from sight, leaving a bloom of blood in the water.

*The clustered houses
of a tundra village
ride out a spring flood.*

At noon they stop to eat and rest, dropping anchor and lighting the little primus stove in the boat to make tea. They share their lunch of smoked dog salmon dipped in seal oil and sprinkled with salt and pilot bread, a hard, round cracker. Jim eats and eats. After months of school cafeteria food—hot dogs for lunch, spaghetti for supper— the native food tastes delicious to him. The men tease him about his huge appetite as they pack away the few remaining bits.

Although there was not much wind when the hunters started at dawn, it is blowing hard now and the water is choppy. Uncle David tells Jim that he can make the next shot, and Jim feels a line of sweat break out on his upper lip. An hour passes, two hours, but there are no opportunities. He knows they are all around him and that he must wait. Then a sleek head breaks the surface of the water only a few yards away. His uncle nods. Jim tries to sight carefully, his breath sucked in, but the heaving boat keeps spoiling his aim. What he wants is a head shot, but the seal is swimming away and Jim knows that he must shoot *now*. He braces himself and squeezes the trigger. Somehow the sound of the shot surprises him, and so does the jerk of the animal's head. He got it! As quickly as they can—the water is rougher and the leads are narrow—they race to the seal and plunge a harpoon into it. It is a large one and Jim has shot it cleanly in the shoulder. Nobody says much, even after they get it into the boat and see the size of it. It would not be like them to show excitement, but Jim can tell they are proud of him. Not long after, David gets a seal too, and they decide to turn back before the weather gets worse.

The return trip is slow. The sea hauls their boat to the crest of each wave and then dashes it into a trough of water, time after time. Spray drenches them, and the harsh wind seems to drive the damp cold into their bones. At last they drag their boat up on the beach, load the seals on the snowmobile sled, and start home.

Jim has been home for two weeks. On the third night his younger brother Pete had awakened him: breakup had begun. They lay in their sleeping bags on the floor and listened to the eerie sounds. For several days the river ice had cracked and heaved, and finally it had begun to move. This was the signal to dig out the boats from under the snow and to put them in the sun to dry. Jim had helped his uncle repair the homemade wooden boat, promising himself that in a few years, when he has his own boat, it will be one of the new aluminum ones, and it will certainly have a more powerful outboard motor than his uncle's. They nailed wooden strips to the bottom as skids and towed it to the beach, an hour's careful trip by snow machine.

Yesterday the men studied the sky and read in it the signs they had been waiting for: a reflection of the sea that told them the shelf ice had broken off and the leads were open. In a few more weeks most of the ice will have moved out to sea, but in April there are still huge floes that can suddenly drift together and crush one of the fragile skiffs. Still, hunting is less dangerous than just before breakup when the men drive their snow machines far out on the ice, risking the chance that a piece might break off and carry away one of the expensive machines or one of the hunters. Sometimes the ice drifts back and the machine or the hunter can be rescued; sometimes not. There have been no hunting fatalities in Chaputnuak for years, although several snow machines lie at the bottom of the Bering Sea, but last year in a village to the north a young man was marooned on the ice for a week. He survived, but both his feet had to be amputated and the ordeal affected his mind.

By now everyone in the village knows that it was a good day and that Jim has gotten his seal. The hunters had sent word to the village by walkie-talkie, and since nearly every home has a citizens' band radio, the word spread quickly from house to house. Liz Koonuk, delighted with the news of her son's success, has begun to plan the celebration. His brother Pete chews on a mixture of excitement and envy.

Pete, just thirteen years old, will not be able to go seal hunting until after the ice clears. Open water is less dangerous, and one of his uncles will invite him to come along then. Only when they are sure he can take care of himself and be a real help will he be allowed to go out for early spring seal hunting.

Pete is already a good shot. Like the other boys his age, he has been shooting at things for more than half his life. When he was small he learned to use a slingshot, and by the time he was six he could pick off an occasional target with an air rifle. At eight he got his first bird, a ptarmigan, and his family celebrated with a big party. Since then he has been helping to supply his mother with birds for the soup pot.

As soon as school was out today, Pete rushed home and picked up his .22 rifle, slung a sack over his shoulder, and started out to meet his friend Mike. But before he could get out the door, his mother reminded him the water supply was low and that this was her washday. There is no running water in the village, and fetching water from the well is a frequent chore. It's a chore Pete likes, though, because it gives him a chance to use his father's snow machine. Pete hooked the wooden sled to the back of the machine, loaded on the empty plastic jerry jugs, and took off for the well at the other end of the village. Some of his friends were already there, filling jugs at the spout. Back home, he emptied the water into the galvanized can in the kitchen and made a second trip to fill his mother's wringer washing machine. Then he was free to hunt ducks.

In April the sky is full of migrating waterfowl, and Pete brought down four ducks without much trouble. Before he and Mike went home, they stopped to visit Mrs. Ivanoff, the oldest woman in the village, and each gave her one of his ducks. Pete is not sure if he is actually related to her, but he and the other boys always take her something when they come back from hunting or gathering eggs. This is not merely a kind gesture; taking food to old women is an ancient custom that supposedly brings luck to young hunters. Mrs. Ivanoff is very deaf, but she weaves beautiful baskets and still goes out on the tundra to gather the grasses for them herself. She thanked the boys for the ducks, and they took the rest home to their mothers. Liz greeted Pete with the news of Jim's seal.

Now Liz cleans the ducks, feeding the entrails to the dog and carefully plucking out the feathers, but everything else, including the feet and head, goes into the pot with water and onions and a handful of rice. She sets the pot on the stove to simmer, and her cooking is done for the day. When Jim returns, she will butcher his seal. Although preparing food for storage is a big job for the village women, cooking it is not. Some food is eaten raw; the rest is boiled with a minimum of fuss.

Pete's sister Louise comes in, a scarf tied over pink plastic curlers. Louise, seventeen, dropped out after one year of high school, like many other girls in the class. Now she helps her mother and her older sister Anna, who has a small baby. Anna's husband Carl was not feeling well, Louise tells her mother, and that's why he did not go out seal hunting with the others. Liz understands that "not feeling well" means "drunk." Anna's house was cold, because the stove had run out of fuel. Carl was over at the pool hall, but he had forbidden Anna ever to come looking for him. So Louise had pumped the fuel for her and gotten the stove going again—a hard job. When the soup is ready, Liz tells her to take some over to her sister.

Louise picks up Evon (his name is pronounced EE-vahn), her youngest brother, and sits down next to six-year-old Mary to watch television. *Sesame Street* flickers uncertainly from the public broadcasting station in Bethel, but Mary watches with rapt attention. She is learning English in school now, and she understands a little of what is being said, especially the numbers. The three of them sit still for the news, first in Eskimo, then in English, broadcast from the Bethel newsroom, but when a four-day-old tape comes on with John Chancellor's earnest delivery of national and world news, Louise goes to comb out her hair. A young man she likes will be coming back with the other hunters, and Louise wants to look nice in case she sees him. Mary follows her. Louise brushes back the little girl's straight black hair and fastens it with a plastic barrette. A few weeks ago she pierced the child's ears, and she puts a pair of her own bead earrings into the holes to replace the wires. Mary touches her new jewelry, smiles broadly—her front teeth are missing—and runs off to show her father.

Charlie Koonuk drinks tea at the kitchen table with Evon on his lap now. Charlie is the maintenance man at the village school, and although he was once a fine hunter and chafes at his lack of freedom, Charlie is one of the fortunate men of the village: he has a steady income.

A few years ago it was neither usual nor important to have a job. But a few years ago in Chaputnuak and the other Eskimo villages of this region, people lived almost entirely on what they could shoot, catch, or forage, and they sold or bartered furs and ivory carvings for the few other things they needed.

Today it is different: cash is essential. There is little wood for fuel, and families burn stove oil to heat their homes. There are no more dog teams; expensive snow machines have replaced them. And while a family no longer has to net two hundred pounds of fish each week to feed a dogteam, gasoline costs money. Tastes have changed, too. Young people don't want to be bothered with heavy fur parkas; they'd rather send for down jackets from mail-order catalogues. These days it is not enough to be a good hunter. You need a job, too.

That is why there were some mixed feelings about Jim's unexpected homecoming. His parents were glad to see him, no question about that. His mother hugged him and made sure he got the choicest pieces from the soup pot that night. His father shook his hand warmly. There was the usual restraint between them, as between every Eskimo father and son, but this time it seemed different. No questions were asked; his father would never interfere. But when Jim told them that he didn't think he would go back at all this spring—school ends the last of May, anyhow—his father had quietly shaken his head. It was good to have him home, but perhaps it would be better if he went back to school. It's good to hunt, but it's also good to have an education. With an education you can earn money.

Money is what matters in the world of white men, of *gussaks,* and it matters more and more to Eskimos, too. Jim has heard the old men of the village talk about what it was like before the gussaks came—missionaries, traders, teachers. It was different then, some say better, because a man knew how to live off the land. Gussak influence is eating into their lives more every year, it seems. But the old men carefully point out that while many things are different and will never again be the old way, others will not change. They still have their language, their stories, their ways of doing things. The white men cannot take anything away that the Eskimos do not choose to give.

The young men think the old men are naive, but they never say so, not to their faces. Among themselves they express their anger and distrust and sometimes hatred of the white man who they feel destroys their culture and offers pathetically little in return.

Liz is feeding the last of the family wash through the electric wringer, and her mind is occupied with plans for a seal party to celebrate Jim's prize. According to the walkie-talkie report, one of the other families got the biggest seal of the hunt—the first big seal of the season requires a special celebration—but she too will put on a party for the women of the village because this is Jim's first large seal. It will cost more than she can afford, but she is virtually required to spend the money, at least a hundred dollars, to avoid gossip and a reputation of stinginess. Besides, seal parties are part of the social tradition of the village. Having a party every time a seal is killed is a way of sharing, and sharing is basic to Eskimo culture.

But there is no more time now to think about it. Ten-year-old Andy has rushed in and announced breathlessly that he and his friends have been watching up by the airstrip, and the hunters are on their way in.

Never has his village looked so good to Jim. Lights

glow from windows all over town. There are thirty-two houses here, a church, a community center, a pool hall, a National Guard building, two stores, and an assortment of fish houses, steam baths, and abandoned privies that lean at rakish angles. At one end of the village and set apart from it is the complex belonging to the Bureau of Indian Affairs, including the school, teachers' living quarters, and a maintenance building. At the other end of the village, rows of white crosses in the village cemetery are lined up next to the airstrip on the highest ground.

Everything.has been built of materials brought in on the summer barges. Some houses, including the Koonuks,' were put up a few years ago by the Alaska State Housing Authority. Charlie Koonuk agreed to pay $2500 for his one-room house, a few dollars a month for twenty years. But he feels that he has been cheated, and he doubts that there will be much left of the house by the time it's paid for. It was poorly constructed of inferior materials with inadequate insulation. It is drafty when the wind blows—as it does most of the time on the tundra—and impossible to keep warm in the dead of winter when the temperature drops and the windchill factor may be eighty degrees below zero.

Construction is difficult on the tundra. The permafrost—frozen subsoil and rock that never thaws—lies a few feet below the spongey surface that freezes in winter and thaws in summer. Houses cannot be set on foundations sunk into the soil but are raised on stilts or wooden skids to keep them above the ground. The freezing and thawing of the surface cause the houses to warp and twist, so that even the most carefully built houses have no square corners or level floors or doors that close properly. The new houses seem worse than the old ones, though, and because they are so hard to heat, Charlie's fuel bill is much higher than it was in his old place, a tarpaper-covered house much smaller than this one. With the help of the village tractor he had dragged his old home from the other end of the village to this new section of state-built homes and converted it into a fish house, a storage shed for his winter supply of dried and frozen fish, seal meat, birds, and other food, and some tools and lumber for projects that he thinks he might get around to someday. Some other families also converted their former homes to fish houses, but for most it was not worth the effort and the houses were torn down.

A few were left where they were, and Charlie's daughter Anna lives in one of them with her husband and baby. It's a poor house, and Carl speaks at times about building them a fancy new one, but most of his talk seems crazy to Charlie. When Carl drinks, which is often, his talk gets even crazier.

Whether built by the state or by individuals, the houses are laid out in much the same way. All are entered through an enclosed porch that faces south, away from the prevailing north winds and accumulating snowdrifts. Here the women keep the fish they are using for the day's meals. In the Koonuks' porch much of the space is taken up by a gleaming new electric freezer. Although it's never plugged in, Liz keeps it stocked with frozen greens and berries. Her washing machine stands on the porch, too, when it's not being used, and Charlie stores his outboard motor here, also.

The house is essentially one large room with partial walls and a storage cabinet to divide the space into eating and sleeping areas. Except for the separate bathroom there are no doors inside the house, partly because the oil-fueled kitchen stove is the only source of heat and partly because Eskimos do not value physical privacy. Small children sleep in the same bed with their parents, and older children share other beds or cots or roll their sleeping bags out on the floor.

There is no plumbing and no running water. Drinking and wash water from the village well is stored in a twenty-gallon garbage can in the house; a basin of water warms near the stove for washing up. Bathrooms in the state-built houses are equipped with bathtubs, because the state once promised water and sewage lines in the village, a promise that has not been kept. Protecting pipes from freezing in the tundra requires special technology; that technology exists, but apparently the funds to provide it do not. While the villagers wait, they use their pipeless bathtubs as storage bins for dirty laundry and other odds and ends.

When the houses were built, each was equipped with a chemical toilet fitted with a charcoal filter and a vent pipe for removing odors. But those toilets quickly broke down; now each family uses an ordinary five-gallon can with a dash of disinfectant. Every day or so one of the men in the family lugs the "honeybucket" out to the river on the north side of the village and heaves the contents onto the ice or into the water. The outhouses scattered around the village were the misbegotten idea of a visiting gussak—no one quite remembers when—and have long since been abandoned.

Electricity is provided by the village generator—when it's working. The man hired by the village council to keep it running says he plans to fly into Bethel with some of the parts to see what can be done about it. Traditionally Eskimos have a reputation for being able to fix almost anything, using their ingenuity and the simplest tools. But there have been some privately expressed opinions that Billy Green may be an exception to that general rule. The council discusses the situation and always comes to the same conclusion: give him another chance. Meanwhile, the generator operates fitfully, and sometimes the houses have electricity and sometimes they do not. A few families have built their own generators and run them for a few hours at night. But the council members say nothing to Billy. They don't, above all, want to hurt his feelings.

Jim's father has come out to help him drag home his seal. Pete and Andy are there, too, full of curiosity. Jim tries not to show how tired he is, but when his mother tells him there is a pot of duck soup in the house, he gladly follows his father to the kitchen table.

Liz has sharpened her *ulu*, the "woman's knife" with its broad rounded blade and a wood handle at the top, and called her sister Cecelia to help with the butchering. Jim placed his shot well, so the whole skin can be used for making boots. Liz slits the seal down the middle from the chin and flenses off the skin and blubber, the underlying layer of fat, in one piece. Next she separates the blubber from the skin, slices it into large strips, and cuts the meat up into big chunks, all to be given out tomorrow at the seal party. Liz's mother cleans the intestines, pouring water through them, a job traditionally taken over by the old women. The intestines will be boiled and eaten, and the flippers will be made into soup. Nothing is wasted.

Louise helps to carry away the chunks of blubber and meat to store on the porch. Although she knows that when she marries it will be part of her job to butcher the seals, she hopes she will be lucky and marry someone who has a regular job, like her father. Then there won't be so many seals to bother with.

In the kitchen Charlie and Jim set the pot of duck soup between them, dipping in with their hands for chunks of meat, spooning up the rich broth. When they finish, Charlie tells his son that he's going to fix a steam bath, a ritual in the villages, especially after a day of hunting. In the old days every Eskimo village in this part of Alaska had a *qasegiq,* a community house where the men gathered for steam baths. Built of sod like the original houses, the *qasegiq* in Chaputnuak disappeared years ago. Now there is a modern community house with glass windows and vinyl-covered floors, a fine place for bingo and dinners, but not for steam baths. And so, many families in the village have built their own small bath houses, crude wooden shacks heated by a fifty-five-gallon fuel drum turned on its side, fitted with a stovepipe, and fueled with whatever is available: driftwood, old rubber tracks from snow machines, rags soaked in oil.

Jim goes to his cousins' house and the boys wait there until the older men have finished their bath. There is room for only four people in the shack, but even if it were larger the young men would not have joined their fathers. In the old *qasegiq* males of all ages gathered to listen to the storytelling of the old men, but in this little hut the ages are kept separate.

The boys stoop to enter the outer room. Lined with soggy cardboard, it is cold and damp, lit by one dim bulb, too low-ceilinged for standing upright. They hang their clothes on nails and crawl on hands and knees through a little door into the steam room. It is nearly dark, illuminated only by the glowing fire. Their fathers had added more fuel before they left, and the tiny room is very hot. Jim sits on the wooden floor facing the stove while his cousin Tony ladles water over the layer of hot stones on top of the drum. The water hisses and steam rises in scalding clouds, filling the room. Jim breathes shallowly, so as not to take the steam into his lungs. In seconds he begins to sweat.

As soon as the steam begins to subside, Tony throws more water on the stones. Suddenly Jim can bear it no longer, and he crawls hastily to the outer room. His cousins follow and sit on the low bench until they have cooled down. Twice more they steam; the last time they wash with

soap and warm water dipped from the drum next to the
fire. All three are short but slim and hard-muscled, their
light brown skin beginning to darken where it is exposed
to the spring sun, their bodies nearly hairless. Jim has few
signs of a beard, although he hopes that he will someday
be able to produce a thick mustache like his uncle Wally's.

They dry and dress slowly, feeling relaxed and sleepy.
Jim has not had the pleasure of a steam bath since the last
time he was home in the village. He has become accustomed to hot showers instead—not bad, but never as good
as this. His cousins congratulate him on the seal he has
killed. You're a pretty good shot, they tell him. We thought
you might have been in Bethel too long and forgotten how
to hunt; that maybe they'd turned you into a gussak.

"They never will," Jim says.

Early the next morning Jim eases quietly out of his
sleeping bag and steps over the curled-up bodies of his
brothers. He moves the coffeepot to a warmer spot on the
stove and spreads Crisco on some pilot bread. While the
coffee heats, Jim zips insulated pants over his jeans and
long underwear and pulls on heavy boots. Between swal-
lows of lukewarm coffee and bites of cracker, he collects
his rifle and ammunition. Then he puts on his down parka
and gloves and goes out to meet his uncles.

During this season while the seals are migrating north,
the men will hunt nearly every day, from daybreak until
late at night. It may be after midnight before they have had
supper and a steam bath and go to bed. Five hours later
they will be up again.

Liz gets up early, too, for she must make preparations

for the seal party. She has decided not to bake any bread, but she will serve her guests *akutaq,* called "Eskimo ice cream" by the gussaks. Traditionally it was made by grating tallow, the hard white fat of reindeer or caribou, and by beating it with seal oil to form a soft, smooth fat, like shortening—so much like shortening in fact that most women use Crisco now instead, which is always available in the village store, while reindeer and caribou are scarce in this part of Alaska. Liz mixes the *akutaq* in a large basin, adding frozen salmon berries and blueberries with a little sugar and canned milk.

Later Liz shops at the store run by the village council. There is nothing fancy about the store: rough shelves around the unpainted walls, a couple of tables in the middle, cartons on the floor. Liz is not the only customer. There will be other seal parties today, but hers is to be first, since Jim is her oldest son and this is his first big seal. She collects the gifts she'll distribute to her guests: canned fruit, crackers, cookies, boxes of cake mix, candy, packets of dried soup, apples, tea bags. Next the useful little items: shoelaces, candles, flashlight batteries, thimbles, matches, sponges. She picks up cans of coffee, and sacks of flour, rice, and sugar to be doled out.

The council store has all the food she needs, but for dry goods she goes to the store owned by Ted Egoak, the sharpest businessman in town. He has the dealership for snow machines and outboard motors, plus the parts for both, and he is by far the wealthiest man in a very poor village. At Egoak's she buys swatches of cotton and corduroy fabric, a mophead, a set of kitchen spoons, a package of underpants, a box of tampons, cards of rickrack trimming, and other items. Then she remembers soap powder and a few cans of snuff. Before Egoak adds up her bill he shows her something very special, flown in yesterday from Bethel: fresh chicken eggs. Like all gussak food in rural Alaska, they are quite expensive, $1.50 a dozen, but she buys three cartons. She does not have cash to pay for all of it; Egoak will add it to her account.

The guests are invited by CB radio, and late in the morning they begin to gather outside Liz's house, perhaps thirty women and a dozen little children. By tradition no men are present—not even the hunter being honored. Inside are her own relatives: her mother, two sisters, two daughters, and a half-dozen aunts, cousins, and nieces. Liz and her sister Cecelia carry the tubs of blubber and seal meat outside, and the party is on. The guests come forward a few at a time, with smiles and greetings, and each gets a share of the seal in her bucket and a portion of *akutaq* in her bowl. When the seal meat and blubber have been distributed, Liz brings out a special bundle, a pillow case containing a red fox pelt, a pair of brightly checked polyester slacks, and a few other choice items. The women crowd together, and Liz throws it up over their heads, hoping that it will be caught by one person and not argued over by several. The bundle drops into the hands of one of the younger women. She is well-liked, and everyone seems satisfied that she is the one to get it.

When Liz and her mother are ready to give out the bulk items—sugar, flour, coffee, rice, and soap powder—

the women surge forward again, this time carrying little bags or squares of plastic. Some of the older women who are wearing *qaspeqs*—cotton covers over their fur parkas —collect each handful in a separate part of the deep ruffle around the bottom of the *qaspeq* and tie it up with pieces of string that Liz had given them.

Liz knows that the eggs will be a great treat. Since it is a ritual to start with the oldest, Mrs. Ivanoff is the first to receive an egg to put in her bucket of seal meat. She cherishes her position as the eldest, but some of the other old women do not like to be singled out.

Then comes the free-for-all. Back up on the steps Liz begins to toss small items out over the heads of the crowd, ending with pieces of cloth, bundles of string, and lengths of yarn. There is nothing restrained about it: the women jump, push, squeal, and grab, except for the old ladies who sit placidly out of the way. Once in a while Liz or Cecelia hands something to each of the elderly women. And then the party, which cost Liz more than one hundred fifty dollars and lasted less than an hour, is over.

But there will be more parties. Word has just come back from the coast that one of the men has shot a walrus. Because of its size—nearly three thousand pounds—the men will butcher it on the spot and bring it back in sections. Walrus has become increasingly rare in this area, and the enormous tusks are prized by the ivory carvers of the village. The hunters' wives are jubilant in their quiet Eskimo way.

May

Louise and Mary walk very slowly, keeping their eyes on the ground, so they will not miss the nests.

Mary scrambles over patches of snow and mounds of vegetation in her hunt for duck, goose, and ptarmigan eggs. A duck explodes upward, wings beating, from the low-growing shrubs just ahead of them, and Louise and Mary hurry toward the spot from which she flew. The tundra is wet and muddy and walking is hard. They search carefully until Mary squeals with excitement: a nest with six eggs in it! Louise helps her put the eggs, nest and all, in her basket.

Suddenly Louise jumps back, startled. She has nearly stepped on a ptarmigan, a kind of grouse with plumage that makes it very hard to spot: in winter its feathers are completely white, but by the middle of May they have turned a mottled brown that blends perfectly with the ground. Not many stay here to lay their eggs; most migrate farther north, although they are land birds and not good flyers. Louise gathers that nest, too. All the eggs are fertile, and later in the season the embryo chicks will be well developed in the eggs they find, but the family will boil them and eat them, embryos and all.

Mary is already an accomplished egg hunter, having found her first nest when she was barely four. There had been a party then to celebrate; the ability to provide food is reason for celebration in every Eskimo village. Sometimes a small child is given a little help in finding eggs for the first time; it is not unknown for a parent or older sister to lead a young child in the direction of a full nest. But soon the children become sharp-eyed and need no adult help.

The sisters do not venture far, because walking on the soggy ground is difficult and tiring for a little girl. Another day Louise will pack a lunch and go egg-hunting with her friends. They will fan out over the tundra, combing the area thoroughly so that no nests are overlooked, no eggs left behind. Next month, when the weather is warmer, the whole family—except for the baby Evon, but including their elderly grandmother—will go by boat to a good nesting area out along the coast.

Last year's trip was a near-disaster. Although daylight lasts nearly around the clock, June is still cold and wet, and they all wore hipboots and raincoats over their parkas for the trip down the river and out along the coast. They had traveled for more than two hours until they found a place to set up camp, using tarpaulins to make a sleeping tent. Then they brewed tea over the camp stove to warm themselves before they started off on foot. The women and children gathered eggs while Charlie and Jim took their rifles and went looking for geese. It was late when they quit, but they cooked the eggs to keep them from breaking and cleaned and boiled the geese. After midnight they lay down in their sleeping bags and listened while the grandmother, Frances Koonuk, told stories for another hour before they fell asleep. In the cold morning, after breakfast in the tent, they loaded their gear into the boat and started out again to try a new area.

But far out along the shore the engine coughed and sputtered and finally died. And it would not start up again, no matter what Charlie and Jim did. When the tide went out, they tied a rope to the front of the boat, climbed into the shallow water and began to drag it across the mud flats while Liz and Louise tried to help by poling the boat. Several hours passed and progress was slow, but at last they managed to maneuver the boat into the broad mouth of the river still miles from their village upstream. Here they stopped to rest, hoping that someone would find them and bring help. No one came. When a fierce storm broke, the family took shelter in the anchored boat, under the tarp. The weather turned bitter cold, and the rain lashed relentlessly. Obviously no help would appear in this weather. Finally, with Jim left in charge of the family, Charlie began the long trek to the village on foot.

Their supply of tea was gone, but Liz divided the last

*A little girl wearing a
traditional* qaspeq
eats a non-traditional breakfast.

of the pilot bread among the children, and everyone ate some of the eggs. There was no way to keep warm enough, but they sang to keep their spirits up, and the grandmother had more stories to tell. They got what sleep they could on the hard bottom of the boat while the storm howled around them and the hours passed slowly.

Meanwhile, Charlie slogged through rain and deep mud for eleven hours. When he arrived in Chaputnuak, wet, hungry, and exhausted, he stopped only long enough to eat and change clothes before he borrowed his brother's boat and started down the river. It was early morning when he reached his cold, miserable family and brought them safely to their own home again.

But there were plenty of eggs left, and they had five geese.

Egg hunting finished for the day, Mary sits down to watch television and Louise pages slowly through the Montgomery Ward catalogue, planning her new wardrobe for summer. She is looking forward to the warm, bright evenings in July when the sun will dip below the horizon for only a couple of hours each night. Then she can dress up and fix her hair and try out some new make-up, which nobody can even notice at this time of year under the coats and hoods and scarves. On her list so far, Louise has a pair of dress shoes to wear indoors and for strolls on the board-walk that serves as the main village thoroughfare plus a pair of tennis shoes for casual wear.

Louise is quite interested in fashion, and like other

girls in the village she does not want to wear traditional Eskimo clothing; in her opinion, that's for old women and children who don't yet know any better. Liz does not attempt to persuade her, for she also has a mail-order wardrobe. Television, movies, the department stores in Bethel, and catalogues from several mail-order companies have given them both a taste for gussak styles. Like everyone else, male and female of all ages, Louise has a warm parka that Liz made for her, skin side out, fur side in for warmth, the hood edged with a wolverine ruff. She also has several colorful *qaspeqs* of bright cotton trimmed with rickrack. The *qaspeq* has a single pocket in the front with room for both hands and whatever she might want to carry there and a ruffle around the bottom that hangs well below her knees. Some of the girls wear the short *qaspeq* as a blouse with slacks, but Louise thinks they look terribly old-fashioned. She much prefers knit tops and blouses that button.

The one nice thing about being at school in Bethel, Louise believes, is that some people there dress better than they do in the village, and you can try on clothes in the department stores. Lots of things are better about Bethel. Sometimes Louise wishes she had not dropped out of school.

Louise had not been particularly interested in school while she was there. She had gone, like the other girls, mostly because everyone else was going. She didn't much care about getting a job, either. Some day, probably, she would get married, but there was no hurry about that. In the meantime she was fairly contented just to stay at home.

When she is feeling restless, she talks about going back to Bethel for one of the job training programs. Or maybe she could go to the Job Corps center in Oregon to learn to be a cook. Then she could get a job in the school lunch program. The pay is more than four dollars an hour, not bad for part-time work. The village is dull; there is nothing to do here. Maybe she'll take a little trip soon. She wishes she could go down to Bristol Bay to the canneries this summer. Lots of older girls are doing that now. She could go next summer when she's eighteen, earn some money, meet some new people. But it's very hard work, and maybe she would be better off to stay at home. She doesn't really know.

That was part of the problem in high school, too: she didn't know what she wanted. Only the boys really seemed to pay attention to their school work; most of the girls just didn't care, and a lot of them ended up in trouble. Some of the girls began to date older boys and young men from the town, usually Eskimos, but occasionally whites. Often they started drinking. Although Bethel is dry and no liquor is sold there legally, many people continue to import it from "wet" cities like Anchorage, or to buy it from boot-leggers. It doesn't take much to get a young girl drunk. Perhaps because the girls are less motivated to learn and less involved with their schoolwork, almost five times as many girls as boys find themselves in trouble of some kind.

Louise was not one of them. But she did not study much either, and her grades were poor from the start. Fi-nally, when the plane came to take the students of Chaputnuak back to Bethel at the start of Louise's sophomore year, she decided at the last minute not to go.

Although there is much to do to help at home, Louise's leisure time passes slowly. She has been learning beadwork, but that doesn't interest her for long. She got a tape player for Christmas, and she collects cassettes of her favorite rock and country singers and listens to them by the hour. She watches television, looks at comic books, pores over the mail-order catalogues, experiments with make-up and hair styles, and plays with Mary and little Evon. And she waits for something to happen.

Chaputnuak seems more alive every day. By the end of May the high school students have come home from Bethel, and it is not yet time for anyone in the village to leave for summer jobs at the fish canneries and on commercial fishing boats. For the men who do not have regular jobs, summer is the time to earn cash. Hours at the canneries and on the boats are long and the work is hard, but the pay is good, and they're sure to earn enough even in a poor season to buy fuel for the following winter and other necessities, too.

Some of the families will move to the fish camp up river near Bethel. But not the Koonuk family. Charlie is an employee of the federal government, since he works at a school run by the Bureau of Indian Affairs (BIA), and he must continue to put in forty hours a week all around the year, except for national holidays and a two-week vacation.

Charlie is well paid—he earns nearly twelve thousand dollars annually—but at certain times of the year he is a restless man. Eskimo culture is based on seasonal activities, with a proper time for each: hunting seals and birds in spring, catching fish in summer and fall, trapping in winter. He feels these rhythms of his natural world, but they do not coincide with the world of a government institution, where he must report every morning at eight, take off exactly one hour for lunch, and stay until five, even if his work is finished. The man who had the job before him did not last long. Like many Eskimos, he was used to sleeping in the morning until he felt rested, and he never paid much attention to the clock. There were days when he felt that he had to go out to hunt seals or to shoot birds, or to check his nets or his traps. He was not "reliable," the gussaks said, and they fired him. Charlie got the job instead. He is reliable, but he is not particularly happy.

In this village of about thirty families, there are perhaps two dozen paying jobs, many of them part-time, nearly all financed by federal, state, regional, or local government agencies. The BIA is the best-paying employer: besides Charlie and the cook, the school hired from the village a bilingual first grade teacher and two teacher aides who took special training courses in order to do paperwork and help some of the students while the regular gussak teachers are busy with other classes. The postmaster is another federal employee, and the twenty members of the National Guard receive monthly checks from the U.S. government. Two health aides are paid by the regional health agency.

With money obtained from various state and federal grant programs and from the frequent bingo games, the village council maintains a payroll that includes a secretary, bookkeeper, two clerks who work in the council store, and maintenance men who tend the community center, parish house, "light plant" (the often-malfunctioning generator), clinic, and village well. Once they hired a man to collect the honeybuckets from each house and empty the sewage into a huge drum, which he was then supposed to haul out on the ice where breakup would eventually "flush" it out to sea. But it was an unpleasant job, and after a couple of weeks he quit and each family went back to emptying its own. The church pays its own maintenance man and bucket-emptier.

Mr. Egoak, the store owner, is the only real entrepreneur in town, but there are other ways of picking up extra money. The women who call the bingo numbers on a Sunday afternoon collect ten dollars for their efforts. The man who shows movies two nights a week at the community center charges admission and hopes that it will cover the cost of the film (Kung Fu movies are sure money-makers, but anything else is risky). Many women weave baskets that command high prices in Anchorage and other cities; a couple of men carve ivory when it is available. Most men trap furs in winter and sell them to the trader in Bethel.

Although wages are well above the U.S. average, prices in this part of Alaska are the highest in the state, and Alaska as a whole has the highest cost of living of any

state. Although it is rich in natural resources, it has virtually no agriculture and little industry. Everything must be
shipped in from the Lower Forty-Eight by plane or boat,
and freight charges often amount to more than the original
cost of the item.

Bethel and Nome, farther north along the Bering Sea
coast, share the distinction of being the cities with the highest supermarket prices in the United States—almost double
the prices in Seattle. At the end of 1975 a ten-pound sack
of flour, for instance, cost about four dollars, and a pound
of hamburger meat about two dollars. A three-pound can
of coffee was $5.81, and ten pounds of sugar was $6.61.

Because all materials must be brought in by barge,
private construction in the bush is expensive. So is maintenance. Stove oil costs about thirty-five dollars per drum,
and families in poorly insulated houses may burn as many
as twenty drums a year—a cost of seven hundred dollars to
heat a one-room house. There are no automobiles to worry
about, but each adult male expects to own a snow machine,
costing from fifteen hundred dollars to two thousand dollars, plus a powerful outboard motor at well over one thousand dollars. Fuel for them is expensive, too. Most long-
distance travel is by plane, and a trip from the village to
Bethel for bank business or a visit to the doctor is thirty
dollars each way.

Unike many other Eskimo villages in Alaska where
jobs are even scarcer, Chaputnuak has only a few families
on welfare and a few more receiving food stamps. It's a
poor town, but nobody goes hungry.

Mary and her cousin Nancy run straight from school to Nancy's house. They smear peanut butter and jelly on pilot bread and gulp down glasses of Tang. Then Nancy finds her story knife in the box under her cot, and the two girls go outside into the mud near the house. It's perfect for storytelling—not too wet, not too dry. They squat down and Nancy smoothes a space in the mud and begins to draw with her knife. First she sketches the layout of a house furnished with rectangles and circles to represent a stove, table, chairs, beds, and wash basin, just like her own home. Then she commences her tale about a little boy who has been playing "string story," even though his parents have told him to stop playing and go to sleep. Mary smiles; she likes this tale because she is good at playing string story herself—knotting a piece of string into a loop and manipulating it on her fingers to form all sorts of complicated figures: the Arrow, for instance, and the Net.

Nancy draws characters in the house—symbols for Mother, Father, and Boy—and describes what is happening in that scene. As she finishes each scene, she erases the drawing from the mud with her hand and sets up a new one. When Nancy's tale is done, Mary takes her turn; she has brought her knife with her in a jacket pocket. Nancy and a friend who has joined them listen intently to Mary's tale of a grandmother who goes out to gather eggs.

Years ago the *yaaruin,* story knife, was carved out of driftwood or walrus tusk by the father for his daughter, who used it to sketch her home, in those days a round sod house with a firepit in the center. Today, as in the past, little girls begin telling knife tales when they are about five, telling more and more complicated stories until they are in their teens. Some of the tales are traditional, but often they make up stories, usually about food-gathering. In old-time Eskimo society knife tales were about hunting, fishing, and foraging. In Chaputnuak and other small villages with a foot in both the old world and the new, at least some of the stories have to do with shopping at the village store. And in modern Bethel, "food-gathering" tales are about Eskimos who drive their cars to the supermarket once a week for groceries.

The stories change, and the designs drawn in the mud have changed, but the language spoken by Mary and her friends is still Yupik. The knife tale is found only in southwestern Alaska, from the Yukon River on the north to Bristol Bay on the south, where Yupik is the dialect.

The territory Eskimos inhabit is enormous, from Alaska through Canada as far east as Greenland, and the population is small and widely scattered, yet the language of all Eskimos is basically similar. Linguists claim that although there are differences in dialect—consonants shifted, vowel sounds altered—Eskimos from southwestern Alaska should theoretically be able to make themselves understood to Eskimos anywhere else. The Eskimos are not linguists, however, and in reality most Yupik Eskimos cannot understand or be understood by the Inupiat Eskimos of northern Alaska.

Before the arrival of the white man in the Arctic, there was no written Eskimo language, although some groups had a form of picture writing. There was, however, a language of gestures, and travelers from one group to another who found they could not communicate by their spoken dialect often relied on hand motions to convey their meaning.

It was the missionaries who brought the Roman alphabet to the Eskimos in the eighteenth century, and from this a written language was eventually derived. Today in Bethel the Yupik Language Workshop has tried to develop consistency in the written language, in which common words are often given a number of highly individual spellings, depending on who is writing it: is it *gussuk* or *gussak?* *kasgek* or *qasegiq?* *kuspuk* or *qaspeq?*

Eskimo is a polysynthetic language in which an enormous number of modifiers can be added, like building blocks, at the end or in the middle (but rarely at the beginning) of a basic word to give it a complete and precise meaning. The result is one very long word that conveys the same meaning as a whole sentence in English. A simple noun may have thirty-six endings; a verb can take more than six hundred forms. Eskimo is far more precise than English or most other European languages: one word, for instance, can describe the exact quality of snow on the tundra at a given moment or the exact location of a seal on the ice.

Yupik is a difficult language for most English-speaking people to master, not because of the complex grammar but because Eskimo sounds are quite different from English sounds. There is a subtlety of pronunciation that English-speaking people often don't catch. Like German,

Eskimo is a gutteral language, with many sounds produced in the throat. But it is not so harsh sounding as German; some people describe it as "juicy."

Mary and Nancy are learning to read and write Yupik in their first grade class. The teacher is Eskimo, but once a day the gussak teacher comes to the small classroom to give the children beginning lessons in English, too. Above the blackboard are two alphabets: first the English alphabet and beneath it the Yupik alphabet, similar to English except that B, D, F, H, J, O, and X are missing.

Traditionally, since there was no written language until recent years, Eskimos are not inclined to be readers. But they have always been storytellers, from childhood on. Little by little, though, the children are learning that good stories can be found in books, too, often with attractive pictures. Soon Mary will be able to read some of these stories to herself in Yupik. Prepared by gussak educators, the stories are only part-Eskimo: one tells about a little girl in a red *qaspeq* who takes a basket of dried fish and *akutaq* to her grandmother and meets up with a wolf; another about an unhappy girl whose selfish sisters treat her badly until she meets a great hunter at a dance, where she manages to lose, not a glass slipper, but her sealskin *mukluk*.

By fifth grade, according to the timetable of the bilingual program, Mary will be able to speak, read, and write equally well in English and Yupik. In reality, though, it will take several more years until she is completely fluent. Mary's parents speak Yupik at home; heavily accented English is reserved for gussak teachers, visiting nurses and doctors, the pilots of the bush planes, and of course, the village priest. Mary's aunt knows English as well as her parents, but she refuses to speak it, ever. The aunt does not like gussaks, and she will not eat their food or speak their language.

Jim and Louise and others their age speak English well. They have been listening to gussak teachers since they were six years old. Jim remembers that he was not allowed to speak Yupik at school when he was in first grade. There was no bilingual program then, and the teachers forced him to speak English, slapping his hands with a ruler if he answered in Yupik. But when he was in third grade a more enlightened teaching couple arrived. They did not punish Yupik, but they rewarded English. Children who remembered to speak only English in their teacher's hearing collected a quarter at the end of the week.

That was in the days when Eskimos as well as whites believed that whatever was gussak was better than what was Eskimo. Jim had tried hard to learn English, and he was ashamed that his parents spoke it so poorly. But gradually a change began to take place. A few years ago Eskimos began to say that they did not want the white man to run their lives completely. They wanted the right to decide which parts of the white world were good enough to keep and which were not. Many times they seemed to have no choice: no one would argue that dependence on alcohol was good, but the Eskimos seem unable to rid themselves of it. One thing they knew they wanted to keep was their language. Eventually the white educators—the BIA and the state-operated schools—began to agree. It ceased to be a disgrace to speak Yupik, and the bilingual program was introduced to preserve it.

Boys never tell knife tales. They play games or go off to shoot birds. And no boy would ever handle a story knife.

There is a superstition that a boy who uses a girl's things will be unlucky in hunting. It is, in fact, a pervasive belief: men do not use women's belongings or do women's work, nor will they permit women to leave their traditional role. Men are considered naturally superior to women, and although women may often have some influence, they have no official voice. Eskimo society is one of strong male domination, and the roles of men and women are strictly defined.

Because of the rigors of Arctic life, survival once depended on these clearly defined roles: every man needed a wife, and every woman needed a husband. Man was the hunter, and hunting required a strength and endurance that women presumably do not have. Furthermore, someone had to prepare the food and clothing from the hunter's catch. It was the man's work to bring home the seal; as soon as it was brought into the porch of the house, it became the property of the woman who skinned and butchered it. She prepared the skin for sewing boots and covering the kayak. And she prepared the meat for cooking, the intestines for sewing into a raincoat or the window of a sod house, the blubber for eating and for the oil lamp that provided light and heat. And, of course, she bore and took care of the children. Without a husband, a woman had no food. Without a wife, a man had no clothing.

In the old days, a hunter considered his wife of little importance as a person, although there may have been a strong emotional bond between them. If a woman tried to harpoon an animal herself, the hunters believed that other animals would stay away and that everyone would starve. In subsistence hunting, luck is as important as skill. Today, Eskimo life is no longer at the survival level. There are other ways, besides hunting, to put food on the table: cash from jobs, food stamps from the government when cash is short; welfare when there is no cash at all. But the old attitudes of male superiority do not die.

This is one of the reasons that Louise did not stay in school. Few Eskimo girls are encouraged to have careers, and there seems little point to their education. Boys, on the other hand, are strongly motivated and greatly encouraged by their parents to finish school and get good jobs. Louise's parents did not advise her to quit, but they did not urge her to stay on. It is assumed that she will help out at home until she marries, and then she will help her husband. Her life will essentially repeat the pattern of her mother's.

Liz Koonuk is contented with her life, but she knows there are some women in the village who are not. Liz has never tried to assert herself in the family, and she takes for granted her subservient role. So does Charlie. There are no beatings and few arguments. When he is angry, there is only silence until the problem resolves itself or is forgotten for the time being.

A few years ago someone suggested that Liz run for parish council, the advisory group at the church. But Charlie said it was not her place to speak among men. It was true that she had many ideas and feelings, but it was also true that when the time came she would probably not be able to stand up in front of everyone and say what was on her mind. Others could do as they wished, but Liz would stay at home with her work.

And so, probably, will Louise.

June

ANNA SITS FORLORNLY ON THE BED, ROCKING HER BABY. The house is a mess: dirty clothes scattered on the floor, dishes stacked in the sink, trash can overflowing with disposable diapers. Her husband Carl is getting ready to leave for Dillingham on Bristol Bay, about two hundred and fifty miles south of Chaputnuak, where he will work at one of the salmon canneries. He may be gone for only a few days or for several weeks during the summer season, depending on the catch. The season last year was poor, and the men worked less than two weeks. To make matters worse, Anna found out later that Carl had lost a lot of his wages in the bunkhouse poker games.

The baby, Christine, is cutting a new tooth, and she's cranky and miserable. Carl stops what he is doing to pick her up. Like all Eskimo men, Carl is very fond of children.

Christine is almost six months old, and Carl wants Anna to become pregnant with a son as soon as possible. He has made it clear that their next child must be a boy; if it turns out to be a girl, he has told her he will give it away.

"Eskimo adoptions" are common practice. Even in a society where babies are generally much wanted and loved and children are considered the most precious of life's riches, nearly every family in the village has at one time or another given away a child—when there was not enough money, or when someone else in the family was sick and needed attention, or when there were just too many small children to be cared for properly. And nearly every family has at some time adopted a child—when one of their own children had died of disease or accident, or when their children were grown and the house seemed empty. Many Eskimos like to adopt a granddaughter to come and live with them and care for them as they get older.

Anna hopes that if she has another girl before a son is born her parents will take it to placate Carl. They had taken Evon from Charlie's brother David, asking for the child even before it was born. It had seemed that Mary was to be their last, and both Liz and Charlie missed having a baby around the house. Both of them have brothers and sisters who were adopted from other relatives. Eskimos are not at all possessive about their children, and they seem to care equally for all of them. The adoptions usually work out well for everyone involved.

Anna has mixed feelings about Carl's leaving. She's afraid that he will again gamble away his earnings or spend

*The king salmon
is a prize catch.*

them on liquor or women. But on the other hand, maybe he will treat her better when he comes back. Carl has been drinking too much lately, and liquor makes him nasty. When he's sober, they get along all right. But when he drinks, he seems to turn into another person. He gets in fights with other young men in the village, and sometimes he seems to go completely crazy, hitting her and smashing things. The house is not much to begin with, but it's worse after one of his drinking bouts. Then he says he's sorry, that he didn't mean any of it, that he can't even remember what he said or did, that it will never happen again. Sometimes he even buys her a present, a new sweater or something for the baby, to make it up to her. But it happens all over again just the same, the next time he drinks.

Even without the drinking bouts, it has been a hard year for them. There was little money, and Carl blew most of it. If her father had not helped them, Anna believes they would not have had money for food stamps; certainly they would have run out of fuel. Christine was born in December, a thin, colicky baby. Even though Christine sleeps in their bed and Anna nursed her often, the baby did not gain weight as she should. Anna wondered if there was something wrong with her milk and on the advice of the health aide weaned her to a bottle, but she is still underweight.

Now Christine has sores on her face and arms. Anna thought it was impetigo, a contagious skin infection that she might have picked up from one of the children who come by often to play with her. But the health aide told

Young women find
summer employment on
a canning barge.

Anna that it is scabies and gave her a skin lotion to kill the nearly invisible mites that burrow under the baby's skin and make her itch, and she instructed Anna to make sure the baby's clothes are kept clean and the bed sheets washed often. Scabies is common in poverty areas where hygiene is poor and where people are in close physical contact, although this is the first such outbreak in Chaputnuak in several years.

Anna asks Carl to move her old washing machine outside the house, as many women do when the weather is warm enough. Someone will have to carry water for her and the baby while Carl is away. Except for the laundry they won't need much. But hauling water is much harder now that the snow is gone and the snow machines have been put away for the season, for the jugs must be carried by hand or in a wheelbarrow. The village council has had a hose laid along the boardwalk for use in summer, but it is too far from Anna's house. She timidly suggests that maybe they can use some of Carl's money to buy their own hose to reach it. Carl informs her he'll need every cent for the new snow machine he plans to get. Surprised, Anna protests that the one he has is working fine. He reminds her that she has nothing to say about it. She cries. He leaves.

Louise knows about Anna's troubles with Carl. She will probably hear more about them, because Anna wants Louise to stay with her and Christine while Carl is away. Louise doesn't mind; she loves to take care of the baby, and it seems like such a long time since Evon was that small.

Eskimo babies are constantly being held, walked,

rocked, cuddled, talked to, bathed, and fed; they are rarely allowed to cry. They sleep with their parents from infancy, not only because of lack of space, but because the parents want to be sure they will know if the baby needs anything during the night. Even if Anna had another room in which to put a crib, she would certainly be criticized by her relatives and other older women of the village until she finally gave in and took the baby back into her own bed. An Eskimo baby's environment is totally loving and secure.

Evon at the age of twenty months still has that same complete security. Although he has walked well for several months, he has only recently been taken outside for strolls on the boardwalk. His mother and sisters watch him carefully, as they do in the house, so that he cannot hurt himself. As he begins to range farther, everyone will keep an eye on him. If Evon gets into trouble as he grows up, he will seldom be spanked or even scolded harshly. Eskimo children are not controlled by rules or disciplined by punishment but by quiet lessons on "how to be good" repeated patiently and as often as necessary. If they want something, it is given to them if possible; their parents believe that a child cannot be "spoiled" too much.

Mary and three of her friends have set up a wooden crate, stocked it with canned goods from Liz's shelves, and are playing storekeeper. Mary asks Liz for a bag of lollipops, and Liz hands it over. The children play quietly, whispering among themselves, a lollipop stick poking out of each mouth. Soon there is a pile of wrappers and sticks, and every pop is gone. Liz collects them and dumps them in the trash, but she says nothing. She does not consider that the large quantity of candy they have eaten might be bad for them; they have enjoyed it. Later, Liz offers them some soup. Three stay, one goes home. The children eat back and forth at each other's homes almost daily. No one needs to ask permission, and all adults act as parents for all children in the village. It's an extended family that offers total security.

Eskimo parents have a good reason for not spanking or slapping their children. They hold the belief, a remnant of their ancient religion, that the soul of a dead relative takes up residence in a newborn infant, who is named for the departed one. To strike a child would be like striking one's beloved old relative.

Andy was given the Eskimo name of Ketunruk, for his father's uncle who died just before Andy was born. Andy, although he is already ten years old, is still much indulged. When he ruins his father's good hunting knife, he is not scolded or punished. His father remembers too fondly the uncle who took him hunting when he was a boy to become angry at his spirit in his own son. Instead of yelling at Andy, he simply points out the damage. Apparently this permissive approach to child-rearing is successful, for Eskimo children are generally well-behaved, soft-spoken, and respectful to their parents and elders.

Before the arrival of the traders and missionaries, an Eskimo was given just one name. But the white men insisted that each person must have both a Christian name and a surname. In most cases the Eskimo name became the family name, and a gussak name was added for baptismal purposes. It took a long while for the family names to be sorted out; each gussak seemed to have a different idea of how it should be done. As a result, the rows of mail boxes in the village post office carry a mixture of names, some distinctly Eskimo, some Russian, some gussak, and some derived from gussak given names, like Billy and Jimmy. But babies are still given Eskimo names as well, and that is what people call each other. Many people in the village have the same Eskimo name. Ketunruk, for example, means simply "son." Panik, a common name for girls, means "daughter." Most names, such as Penguk (hill) and Chank (grass) can be given to both boys and girls. People know who is being referred to in conversation by the inflection of the voice, if not the context.

June 22 is the summer solstice. In the rest of the United States this marks the first day of summer, the day with the most hours of daylight. But here in Chaputnuak, as elsewhere in the Arctic, the days of summer are literally endless. For a few weeks before and after the solstice, the sun does not set; it merely dips toward the sea, rolls along the northern horizon behind the village, and then climbs the sky again. The continuous daylight seems to make people more active, less inclined to sleep. Often the children are playing outside until midnight or later; they sleep for a few hours and then rush outside again. The weather is not particularly warm; although the sun is bright and hot, a chilling wind blows continually. Most people wear sweaters or jackets, but the children have taken off their boots and sneakers and run barefoot. Mary comes in covered with mud; Liz wipes her off but does not bother to change her clothes—she will soon be dirty again.

Liz's mother, Amelia, comes to take Mary out to gather greens. Tender new growth covers the tundra, and the women and the girls and young children have begun their foraging trips. What was once a dead white landscape is now alive with low-growing vegetation, much of it important to the villagers' diet. All through the summer they will gather the green plants: willow leaves, wild celery, sour dock, wild rhubarb, ferns, wild spinach. Grandmother is looking especially for a kind of grass that is slit open first to remove the scallion-like center; then she will braid the outside sheath and use it to string up fish for drying.

As they walk, Grandmother talks to Mary about the different kinds of wildlife they see. Amelia knows the name of every bird in the sky, as well as its habits, but she is less sure about the plants. She simply knows which are good to eat and which are not. In the fall she'll be back again, looking for mouse holes. The field mice, too, are busy foraging and hoarding, and the old women are especially good at spotting their cache of *masu,* the tiny roots of various plants that make such good soup and *akutaq.* Back home again with their baskets filled, Grandmother and Mary sit on the steps to rest and to eat a little of the wild celery, dipped in seal oil and sprinkled with salt. Some of the greens will be eaten fresh, and some will be lightly boiled and then preserved in seal oil for winter food.

Not only the tundra has changed with the coming of summer. So have the rivers and creeks, the lakes and ponds.

The waters teem with fish and water life. The mighty king salmon have begun their struggle upstream to the headwaters of the rivers to spawn. When they leave the ocean they are strong and weigh close to twenty pounds, but the fight against the current for hundreds of miles batters and weakens them. Once in the headwaters they lay their eggs and die, their life cycle complete; the young salmon hatch and swim down to the sea. Some of them live for as long as nine years, feeding on the ocean floor before they return to their own river to spawn. They swim near the riverbanks, avoiding the main force of the current and resting in the eddies. In these shallow eddies where the current swirls back upon itself, the Eskimos set their nets, checking them twice a day to collect the fish—ocean fish like flounder, whitefish, and herring that swim in the broad mouth of the river, as well as several varieties of salmon—that have been caught there.

Liz Koonuk and her sister-in-law, Martha, prepare their *ulus* for the day's catch. Charlie, home from school where he has been tending to minor repairs, lugs tubs of fish from his boat to where they're working. Liz and Martha perform as a team: Liz scales the fish, slits it open, and throws the innards into a bucket. Then she passes the cleaned fish to Martha, who deftly fillets it, leaving the pieces connected at the tail to hang over the fish rack. All around the village teams of women squat for hours, working steadily until the pile of fresh fish is gone and racks outside each house are crowded with fish hung up to dry.

Early in June a few families left for the fish camp near Bethel. In the old days, entire village populations moved to fish camp in the summer; it was an opportunity to visit with friends and relatives from other villages and a chance to share both the work and the results of it. Today most men try to find paying jobs in summer, and the women and children stay at home in the village. Salmon fishing is a major industry in Alaska. Toward the middle of June the men with jobs on commercial fishing boats leave for Bristol Bay or Bethel; the men who are not on the boats start work at the end of the month in the canneries that buy the catch.

Thirteen-year-old Pete Koonuk was with the first group of men to go. His uncle David is the captain of a large fishing boat, a sixty thousand dollar vessel equipped with hydraulically operated nets for hauling in the salmon. As captain he can pick his own crew, and he thought the time had come for Pete to get away from the village for the summer. The situation created some gossip, though: Pete's father has one of the best-paying jobs in town, and his brother Jim and brother-in-law Carl are both going to the cannery in Dillingham. Is that not enough income for one family? Would it not be better to hire someone from a less fortunate family?

But David and Charlie ignored the talk, and Pete went. Families always stick together. If a man is in a position to give work to someone else in the village, he will certainly offer it to a close relative. Such nepotism helps to perpetuate a class structure in the village: families that "have" tend to keep on getting, and those that have not are caught in an endless cycle of poverty—even in a culture in which sharing is so important.

Some of the village high school kids who are left behind will have a chance to earn money through the Neighborhood Youth Corps, working four hours a day doing odd jobs like painting the community center and fixing the boardwalk. NYC hires them for six weeks and pays them about two dollars and fifty cents an hour, half the money provided by the state, the rest put up by the village council. Most of the workers will turn their wages over to their families. It's not a major source of income, but it helps, and it gives them something useful to do.

Andy and his grandfather are going muskrat hunting. It's a chance to get some skins to sell, and—just as important—a lesson in shooting and gun safety for Andy. They pack overnight provisions into Grandfather Koonuk's boat: tarps for making a tent, a stove for brewing tea, a supply of food, and of course the guns and ammunition. Late one morning they start up the river to one of the lakes where Grandfather says there will be plenty of muskrats. It's a long trip, but after they have found a high and fairly dry place to set up the camp and have fixed tea and had a bite to eat, they start the tiring walk over the marshy tundra to the first pond that Grandfather wants to visit. The old man has brought his own gun and a .22 rifle for Andy to use. Andy guesses that if he does exactly as he is told and handles the rifle well, his grandfather might let him keep it.

The muskrats begin to come out of their holes late in the afternoon, and Andy sees them swimming out on the pond, rippling the still surface of the water. His grandfather makes a sign: go ahead and try. Andy picks one closest to him, squints along the rifle barrel, and squeezes off a shot. The bullet skips into the water to the left of the muskrat, and immediately there are no more muskrats to be seen. Grandfather touches Andy's arm: it's all right. They'll be back. We have plenty of time.

Andy tries several more shots; no luck. He is angry with himself, but his grandfather keeps reassuring him. He is handling the gun well. Just as important, he is concealing his frustration. The right opportunity will come if he has patience. Then Grandfather shoots, and soon there are a few dead muskrats in the game bag, almost as many as there were shots fired. They stop to eat. Andy is disappointed in his luck and beginning to get tired, but he does his best not to show it. After they have rested, they start off again.

Andy is too anxious now, and when he spots a muskrat he raises his rifle and fires carelessly, missing again. His grandfather shakes his head and begins to tell him a story about the dangers of guns. Andy is restless—he simply wants a chance to shoot—but he respects his grandfather and listens anyway. Once there was a man who shot his best friend accidentally when they were out hunting together. The man was so upset by what he had done that he vowed never to hunt again. As a result, two families were poor and without food: the family of the dead man, and the family of the man who would no longer hunt. There have been other cases like that one, but not many. One must be careful.

While they wait, Grandfather lectures Andy about safety. Like most young Eskimos, Andy does not argue or talk back. Often the young boys do not agree with their elders' advice, and when they are older they go ahead and do as they want—except when it comes to survival and living off the land. The older generation may not understand the new world, but they know everything there is to know about the old world, and the young men listen to them and accept their experience and wisdom without question.

Soon Andy's luck improves. They hunt through the sunlit night, and by the time they return to camp early the next morning Andy is so exhausted that he feels he cannot put one foot in front of the other. Even though they rest before they start home again, Andy sleeps the whole way in the boat, still holding the rifle that is now his. There are fifteen dead muskrats for Grandmother to skin out, three of them Andy's. The pelts will bring them a little money, although not as much as the mink and fox they will trap next winter. Grandmother will use some of the fur to trim the new parka she is planning to make for Mary.

Their work finished, the women gather along the boardwalk and watch the late evening sun shimmer on the pond and cast long shadows on the tundra. They talk quietly, aware of the many sounds around them. The air whirs with the wingbeats of geese, ducks, gulls, terns, and ptarmigans. Shouts drift from the wooden deck outside the school where the younger boys play basketball. Louise and her friends giggle and talk about boys, mostly the ones who aren't here. Old men come out of the steam baths, their wrinkled skin shiny with sweat, and sit naked on the grass to cool off. No one goes to bed before midnight. Time enough to sleep in the long, dark winter.

July

IT'S THE FOURTH OF JULY, AND THE PEOPLE OF CHAPUT-nuak are going to have a good time, once somebody gets around to organizing it. In the villages this strictly American holiday is traditionally a day for races and games with prizes, free treats, and a free movie.

Charlie Koonuk is the logical person to do the organizing: for one thing, he's a member of the village council and has official status; for another, he's one of the few younger men in town at this time of year. Charlie visits two or three of the older council members who will help him buy prizes from the village store, using money alloted by the council for the occasion and donated by people in the village. First prizes will be cash—five dollars for the running races, and so on—but they need lots of smaller prizes, like candy bars and boxes of Crackerjack, so that each child who participates will get something. They also buy soft drinks for everybody and a few dozen oranges to give away.

Most of the contests and races have their roots in competitions that once took place in the *qasegiq,* the community house. A few of the old people still remember what a *qasegiq* was like. There has never been one in Chaputnuak at its present location, but fifty years ago when the village was located a few miles further up the river, Mrs. Ivanoff, the oldest person in the village, helped to build one. Everyone had a part in the construction. Like the individual sod houses, it was partially underground, and the first job was to excavate a pit. Then the men and boys collected logs that had drifted down the river and set them in place, upright posts at the corners, whole and split logs arranged across them to support the roof. The women and children gathered grasses which the old women wove into mats to lay over the logs to keep loose dirt from seeping through. The men packed blocks of sod over the structure, and the women topped that with moss. Soon grass and weeds began to grow on the earth covering, helping to hold it together. In the middle of the *qasegiq* was the fire pit; directly above it a hole in the roof served as a window and an air vent for smoke. There was a summer entrance in the side of the building and a winter entrance through an underground tunnel.

The *qasegiq* served a number of important functions. It was a place for meetings and for dancing and storytelling. It was a bathhouse. It was also home for most of the men and boys of the village who slept there and were brought food by the women and girls who stayed at home to prepare food and clothing. Here the young boys were trained by the old men, who told their hunting stories and taught them to make tools and to build kayaks and traps.

When nothing else was going on there, the *qasegiq* was a kind of gymnasium where young people competed in sports. Many of the men's contests had to do with strength and agility, the kind required of hunters. There were tests of finger strength, for instance, and arm, leg, and neck strength. There was an event called the standing kick in which the contestant leaped up to kick a sealskin bladder suspended overhead. After each try, the bladder was raised higher; to qualify, both feet had to hit it together. The standing kick is still an athletic specialty of many young Eskimo men, although the bladder has been replaced by a large rubber ball.

Sometimes the women's contests were held in the *qasegiq*. Some of them tested their ability to escape from pursuing men. But nowadays, the women who race down the Chaputnuak airstrip are not practicing a getaway from unwanted suitors; they simply like to run. One of the favorite Fourth of July contests is the old women's foot race, in which they prove that although they may carry many years on their backs, their legs are still strong and fast.

Andy and his friends are good runners, too, and they enjoy their own races. But Andy's favorite sport is wrestling, and he has tried—without success—to convince his father that wrestling ought to be one of the Fourth of July contests. During the past winter his school wrestling team

Eskimo girls compete
to determine who
has the stronger neck.

traveled twenty miles by snowmobile and sled to a meet in the next village. Andy was a winner in the fourth-grade group, and he came home proudly displaying the Polaroid snapshot taken by his teacher-coach that shows him pinning his opponent to the mat.

There was a time when games were played without the pressure to win that exists today. The point of most games and contests was not so much to beat someone else but to beat one's own previous attempt. When the white teacher introduced football, for example, the children enjoyed kicking the ball around, but they applauded each other's ability rather than forming teams. They've changed traditional American baseball to suit their own ideas, too, getting a player "out" by hitting him with the ball as he runs the bases.

Most Eskimo children do not have store-bought play equipment. Their homemade toys are often the kind that help develop specific skills. The children spend a lot of time on the seesaw on the playdeck outside the school. Standing on the ends and trying to bounce each other off is an exercise that helps them learn the balance they'll need when they're out hunting in the boats. Andy is especially adept at the can game. His friend holds an evaporated milk can with a half-dozen holes punched in the lid while Andy flips a short stick in the air and hopes it will fall through a hole and into the can. Moving the can is against the rules, and the can-holder who breaks the rule earns a swat.

One of Mary's favorite toys was made for her by her grandmother. Two small balls of sealskin are attached to

*Two boys test
the strength of
their left legs.*

the ends of a leather thong. Mary holds the thong just off center and starts one ball rotating clockwise in front of her. Once it is moving, she starts the other ball rotating in the opposite direction. By an easy motion of her wrist, she can keep the two balls describing circles for quite a long time. These "Eskimo yo-yos" as the gussaks call them are popular items in souvenir shops that sell to tourists.

It's about ten o'clock when everyone begins to gather at the end of the village for the Fourth of July contests. There will be no standing kick—the young men who do it so well are all away working—but there is race after race, for different ages and different sexes. The winner of the old women's footrace is a favorite grandmother who wins nearly every year, and her victory is greeted by cheers. The children run, the old men run. When the races are over, Charlie tries a new idea he's heard about. Liz has made him some hard-boiled eggs, and he passes out one to each of the contestants—no restrictions as to sex and age. The idea is to peel the egg and eat it as fast as possible; the first person to whistle is declared the winner. There is much encouragement of the seven contestants who wolf down their egg, and the winner—to everyone's pleasure—is a retarded woman who beams her delight at her family and friends and collects her candy-bar prize.

The games go on for a couple of hours and end with a tug of war between the men and women. Even though there are fewer men, they easily defeat the women. Then everyone goes home for lunch and a rest.

This year the council voted to have a dinner at the community center, and late in the afternoon each family carries some food to the big hall. The council has provided free soda for dinner, too, and a rare dessert treat: gussak ice cream, flown out from the supermarket in Bethel. In previous years fresh fruit was the special holiday dessert, and the diners congratulate Charlie on his original idea.

When the remains of the food have been cleared away, Charlie sets up the movie projector while one of the other men arranges the chairs in a row. Everybody was hoping for a Kung-Fu movie, but Charlie was rather late in sending in his order and the other villages had all signed up for the available Kung-Fu films well in advance. What Charlie could get is a Walt Disney picture that the villagers have seen before, but they are prepared to enjoy it again, especially since it's free. The kids sprawl on the floor close to the screen, their parents sitting or standing in the back of the hall.

When the movie is finished, no one is in a hurry to go home. The adults talk and watch the children skipping stones over the smooth water of the pond. Charlie is pleased with the way things have gone. People obviously enjoyed themselves. It was a bang-up Fourth of July—maybe the best ever in Chaputnuak.

What the Fourth of July was *not*, anywhere in village Alaska, was a celebration of American freedom and independence. Eskimo children are taught American history in school, of course. They have been rehearsed in the names of George Washington and the other Founding Fathers. They have heard stories about Betsy Ross, the Liberty Bell, Paul Revere, the Declaration of Independence, the American Revolution. But for most of these children, American history is as remote as the study of European geography. And most of the adult villagers would be hard pressed to say exactly what the Fourth of July does commemorate.

And so there was no patriotic observance of the day: no flags flying (not even at the school, since it's not in session), no red-white-and-blue bunting, no speeches, no bands. The Fourth of July in its true meaning has nothing to do with Eskimos, and the history of the United States touches them in only the most remote ways.

It was the Russians from the west, not the European settlers of the American colonies, who were first to reach Alaska. Czar Peter the Great hired a Danish sea captain, Vitus Bering, to explore far northeastern Siberia. By 1728 Bering managed to get his men and supplies across the vast Asian continent and set out from Siberia on his first mission. Although he sailed through the narrow strait that separates the two continents and now bears his name, he did not see the North American mainland. However, in 1741, Bering and his crew tried again, this time with more success for the Russians: they sighted the St. Elias Mountains in the northern part of Alaska's panhandle, called simply Southeastern. Bering, unfortunately, was not the one to carry the news to the Czar; his ship was wrecked and he died on an island in the sea that was also named for him. It was a German biologist on the ship, Georg W. Steller, whose knowledge of edible plants and marine life enabled some of the crew to survive and to return home with news of the discovery.

The voyagers' collection of sea otter skins triggered

the "fur rush" of Russian traders to the Aleutians. The traders took what territory they wanted and exchanged trinkets for a wealth of furs. Terrible stories have been told of Russian treatment of the native peoples. Whole populations of some of the Aleutian Islands were wiped out.

The first permanent settlement of whites in Alaska was established on Kodiak Island, southwest of what is now Anchorage, in 1784. Aleksandr Baranov, managing agent of the Russian American Company, a fur-trading enterprise on Kodiak, became the most influential man in Alaska. Sitka was established by him in 1799 as the first capital, on one of the group of islands that is part of Southeastern. Three years later Tlingit Indians destroyed the capital. Although it was rebuilt, Sitka did not thrive, and gradually Russian interests in Alaska began to decline. Finally, in 1867, Russia sold Alaska to the United States, which bought it at the urging of Secretary of State William H. Seward for $7,200,000. The contract of purchase stated, "the uncivilized tribes will be subject to such laws and regulations as the United States may from time to time adopt in regard to aboriginal tribes of that country."

At first no one knew what to do with this enormous piece of real estate equivalent to one-fifth the land area of the continental United States and long known as "Seward's folly." Initially the Army was officially responsible but neglected it; then the Navy took over and did little better. When gold was discovered around Juneau in 1880, a governor was finally appointed, and in the early 1900s the capital was moved to Juneau. But Juneau's remoteness from the rest of Alaska in both geography and climate became a source of controversy. In 1976, while the rest of the United States was absorbed in electing a new president, Alaskan voters were deciding on a question that may have more immediate impact on their lives: the selection of a place to develop a new capital city. Of the three proposed sites in the same general area, they chose Willow South, a forested area, forty air miles north of Anchorage and about four hundred miles east of Bethel.

Although a century ago most people saw little use for this cold, isolated land, the missionaries recognized it as an area greatly in need of their efforts. Here were pagan souls to be saved, unwashed bodies to be introduced to soap and water, childlike minds to be schooled in the civilized ways of white men. The missionaries began to arrive in the late 1870s, and their influence was considerable. In the process of conversion, the missionaries of some church groups felt they had to stamp out much of the Eskimo culture that they said was getting in the way of Christianizing and educating the natives. This meant that the native language was discouraged and certain customs, such as Eskimo dancing, were banned. In some places ivory carving was prohibited, because the images reminded the missionaries of the old religion they were trying to eliminate.

Not all missionary activity was negative. Sheldon Jackson, a Presbyterian, established schools all through the territory and was later appointed the first federal superintendent for public instruction in Alaska. His interests extended beyond religion and education; he was concerned

about economics, too. Seeing how the wanton destruction
of fur seals by greedy traders had caused great hardship to
the Eskimos, in 1892 with government aid, Jackson brought
the first Siberian reindeer to Alaska and established reindeer herding as a way of making a living.

By the end of the nineteenth century there were dozens of missions all through the territory, many of them du-
plicating each other's efforts. Jackson's solution was to divide the area among the Protestant churches involved: each
of the major denominations cut a piece of the Indian and
Eskimo "pie." The Moravian Church took over the area of
the Kuskokwim River. The Roman Catholic and Russian
Orthodox Churches, not consulted by Jackson's planners,
established themselves in certain isolated villages. Although
Bethel and most of the villages around it are Moravian,
Chaputnuak is one of a group of Catholic villages near the
sea, and there are Russian Orthodox villages further up
river. Although the Moravians do not seek converts where
another church has already established itself, there is again
today considerable duplication, and many tiny villages
have more than one church.

About 1929 some of the more sophisticated villages,
especially in Southeastern Alaska—which has always been
more "advanced" than the bush—began to incorporate as
cities. When World War II broke out, Alaska suddenly
became an extremely vulnerable part of America. The Eskimos, who had been made U.S. citizens in 1924, united
and formed a branch of the Territorial National Guard.
They also helped build U.S. air bases and taught white

military men how to survive in the Arctic. In 1945, the Alaska legislature passed a nondiscrimination act, the first under the United States flag.

Alaska was finally "discovered." Between 1950 and 1960 the population doubled, and on January 3, 1959, Alaska was admitted as the forty-ninth state.

Being represented by one of the stars on the flag outside the BIA schoolhouse does not mean much to an Eskimo living in Chaputnuak or any other isolated village in the bush. His contact with the government is through the agencies that do things for him: the Bureau of Indian Affairs instructs his children; the Public Health Service treats the diseases such as tuberculosis and venereal diseases that were introduced by the white man in the first place; welfare agencies and food stamp programs help to feed his family as the economy continues to shift away from subsistence hunting and fishing to cash. But he feels that the government really knows very little about him and cares less. Although local representatives are hard-working and dedicated, many Eskimos believe state officials are out of touch with the needs and feelings of people in the bush. Washington, D.C., might as well be on the moon.

Summer is tourist season in many parts of Alaska, and white visitors pour into the state from all over the country. Some drive all the way from the Lower Forty-Eight through Canada on the Alaska Highway. Once in Alaska, though, they can't go far on wheels, because highways do not extend deep into the interior. (There are fewer highway miles in Alaska than in the relatively tiny state of Vermont.) Many people cruise by ship through the islands of the Alexander Archipelago in Southeastern. Thousands visit Mt. McKinley National Park, to see or to climb the highest peak in North America. Hunters and fishermen come in droves; so do hikers, campers, and people who love the wilderness. But only a few ever visit coastal Alaska to admire the spectacular colors of the tundra; most of them are on guided tours for a glimpse of native life.

All encounter the summer siege of mosquitoes. Huge, numerous, and voracious, they are the plague of many summer visitors from the Outside (as the rest of the world that is not Alaska is called). They go home with tales of mosquitoes in clouds so thick they obscure vision, invade one's mouth and nose, drop into one's soup. The trick is not to eradicate them but to ignore them, as the Eskimos do. They are an important part of the ecology in this area, a National Wildlife Refuge and one of the most important bird breeding areas of the continent. The insects' life cycle corresponds with the life of the birds that have just hatched and need huge quantities of them for food. When the nestlings are on their own, the mosquito season ends.

Eskimo children aren't much bothered by mosquitoes. Mary catches them by the handful to feed her pet baby gull. Grandmother brought her the gull egg, and for weeks Mary kept it warm near the kitchen stove. One day recently she heard a tapping sound, and within a few hours the shell had broken open and the little gull had stuck out its fuzzy head. Andy used to hatch a gull each summer for a pet, but something always happened to it: a dog got it, or one of the children accidentally brought it down with a sling shot, or it flew away. But Mary is delighted with the fluffy little bird that she can hold in her two hands. She carries it with her to show her friends who have gathered on the boardwalk.

In a few short weeks the chill winds will begin to blow again from the north, and the village Eskimos will begin their preparations for the long months of cold, dark days ahead. But for now the villagers of all ages want to enjoy every hour of warmth and daylight. It is past midnight when the children stop their play and their mothers call them inside for a few hours of sleep.

August

IT'S A DIRTY, SMELLY JOB, CLEANING OUT THE FIFTY-FIVE-gallon drums for stove oil and gasoline. If it weren't for the excitement of the barge due any day with the entire year's supplies and the chance to get paid to help unload it, Jim would tackle the job with considerable distaste. But he really needs to earn some cash.

Jim came back from the cannery in Dillingham a couple of weeks ago. It had been an excellent season, and Jim was able to pile up quite a bit of money. He saved nearly all of it, too, until the end. He stayed away from the bunkhouse poker games, where a lot of cash changed hands, and although he met boys and girls his own age, he didn't go out with them much. Then, when he was ready to leave for home, a couple of his friends got the idea of spending a few days in Anchorage, just to see the sights. His friend

Ed assured him that they could all stay with his relatives in the city and probably eat with them too. He would need to spend very little. It was a temptation he couldn't resist. Wallet bulging with more cash than he had ever seen at one time, he flew to Anchorage.

Getting used to the contrast between the big town of Bethel and his own tiny village and reading about U.S. cities in social studies courses at school had in no way prepared Jim for the city of Anchorage. With an area population of 180,000, the city is a sprawling checkerboard laid out on the flat plain between the majestic Chugach Mountains and Cook Inlet, an arm of the Pacific Ocean. Originally settled by whites and until recently almost exclusively a white man's city, Anchorage is today considered by some the largest native settlement in Alaska, with Fairbanks running second. The native population of Anchorage—Eskimos, Indians, and Aleuts (a distinct ethnic group from the Aleutian Islands)—is about ten thousand, 5½ percent of the city's total population.

Anchorage was a shock to Jim, but it was also exciting. For two days he and his friends hung around Fourth Avenue, the neon-lit midtown strip that lures most village Alaskans who come to the big city for a good time. Avoiding the native bars that attract older visitors, the boys wandered from diner to cheap restaurant to fast-food shop, consuming great quantities of hamburgers, hot dogs, pizza, and milk shakes. At the end of the first day, they took a taxi to the home of Ed's relatives in a low-income housing project. Undaunted by their eating binge, they sat on the

*The barge brings
a year's supplies
to villages on the river.*

floor in the crowded apartment and ate smoked fish that had been sent by mail to the Anchorage Eskimos from relatives in the bush. And the next day they went back to Fourth Avenue again, this time working the other side of the street.

Jim's friend Ed, who had been to Anchorage once before and regards himself as an old hand at city life, announced that he plans to come to live in the city when he finishes school in Bethel. He will get a job doing some kind of electronics work and live in a fine apartment. Some day he'll have a car and be able to go to movies and stroll down Fourth Avenue every night. It's a popular dream among village Eskimos, and many of them try it. They go to Anchorage or Fairbanks where jobs are scarce and often find themselves living in the poor native sections under worse conditions than they ever experienced in the bush. Sometimes they go Outside to the Lower Forty-Eight and work in Seattle on fishing boats or get jobs in factories in Los Angeles and Detroit. But noise, traffic, and crowds disturb them, and they dislike the climate and the fast pace and pressure to watch the clock. They get homesick and return to their villages again. Unable to adapt to subsistence hunting and fishing, many of them wind up collecting welfare.

Past the "native" blocks of Fourth Avenue, Jim saw hundreds of well-dressed white tourists emerging from the modern high-rise hotels, poking in and out of the souvenir shops. In a store window he saw baskets like the ones his grandmother makes, with price tags that made his jaw drop: a couple of hundred dollars, some of them—more than twice as much as she gets when she sends them to a dealer. Why did the store get so much and his grandmother so little? Jim wondered. Ed shrugged; he didn't know either. But it was common knowledge—and a common complaint—that this is what happened to native craftsmen. They thought they were paid well, until they learned how much the shops in Anchorage were asking, and getting, for items with a "Handmade by Eskimos" tag. The concept of overhead—that the shop owner has fixed expenses and also wants to make a profit—is not easily understood by bush natives unfamiliar with business procedures.

Jim wanted to see more of the city, and he briefly considered getting on one of the city buses just to see where it went. But he had never been on a bus, and he was afraid of ending up lost. It was one thing to be out on the tundra alone in a winter storm with whiteness in every direction; that could be coped with. But several lanes of cars, traffic lights, and a bus headed who-knew-where among the huge buildings and endless streets were something else. He decided not to try.

Then one of the taxis cruising on Fourth Avenue presented an alternative. The driver motioned Jim over and offered him and his friends a personal tour of the city. The friends were not interested; Jim decided, with a show of bravado, to go alone. The "tour" was indeed an extensive one. They drove up one street and down the next, from the rich white neighborhoods by the water to the most desolate native slums. At one point the driver showed Jim a bright pink house that advertised itself as a massage parlor but was actually a house of prostitution and offered to wait if Jim wanted to stop. Jim, relieved that his friends weren't there to witness his embarrassment, said no.

That was one of the few points of interest identified by the guide. Jim stopped trying to look and began to worry about how this was going to end. Two hours later the driver charged him sixty dollars for the "tour." Weary and numb, Jim paid him off, nearly weeping at having spent so much and gotten so little. The driver took him back to Fourth Avenue. That night his friends bought a bottle, and Jim got drunk for the first time in his life.

The next day, bewildered, exhausted, and hung over, Jim boarded the jet to Bethel; a few hours later he crawled out of the cramped seat of a plane in Chaputnuak.

Homecoming was a relief. While his family clustered around him, Jim distributed the gifts he had bought: a plate with a painting of Mt. McKinley for his mother, silk scarves with pictures of the state flower, forget-me-not, for Louise and Anna, penknives for his brothers, a tiny plastic purse for Mary, a gussak-looking hat for his father. He would do almost anything to avoid telling his father about the expensive taxi ride.

Happy as they were to see him again, there was a touch of sadness to this homecoming, because they knew he wouldn't be there for long. At the end of the month Jim will be going back to school again. Although his teachers did not fail him for having left in the spring at the beginning of seal hunting, his grades were very low, and he knows that he will be far behind when he enters his classes this fall. But he and his father had talked briefly before he left for the cannery, and Charlie had said that it would please him very much if his oldest son graduated from high school. Charlie didn't say he *had* to go back to school, but Jim knows it's important to his father that he finish.

Nine more months of school; then he can do what he wants. The problem is, he doesn't really have a clear idea of what he wants. In a way he envies his friend Ed who has decided to go to Anchorage. What an exciting place the city is! The memory of the disastrous taxi ride is already beginning to fade. But would he really want to live there? Fourth Avenue was fun, but what about seal hunting, what about fishing and trapping?

Yet if he comes back to Chaputnuak to live, what then? He can do all those things he wants to do, to live off the land as his ancestors did, but will he be able to earn enough money with summer jobs at the cannery? There are always office jobs becoming available in the village, but he doesn't think he would like that: too confining, too boring, just sitting at a desk all day.

And Chaputnuak is not the liveliest place in the world. Maybe he'd go some place really different: Chicago, Illinois; Detroit, to the automobile factories; maybe even southern California. But then he remembered how he felt about a simple thing like getting on a bus in Anchorage, where there were even some other Eskimos, and he realized he'd never go. He watched his mother set the plate on a shelf to show it off, watched his little sister parade with her new purse. Women were so lucky, he thought. They didn't have problems like this—or of having to admit to his father what had happened to a big chunk of his summer earnings. (Later, when he told Charlie, his father looked pained but said only, "Such things happen.")

Soon the fall weather will sweep down on them— cold, rainy, windy—and people will spend more time indoors. But now everyone is outside as much as possible. Pete and Andy go off together in their father's boat to collect driftwood near the mouth of the river. Driftwood is valuable for so many things: some of the big pieces for building projects, the small ones for fuel in the steam baths.

Charlie Koonuk has been talking again about moving his house, using the large pieces of driftwood for skids. It's low and marshy where the house is now, and he has thought of moving nearer the airstrip where the ground is higher and somewhat drier and the mosquitoes not quite so thick. Liz, however, has heard this talk before, and she has not bothered to pack up her dishes or to start taking down pictures from the walls. Moving a house is a huge job, and in all probability Charlie will debate it for a few weeks and reach his customary decision: "Maybe next year."

Charlie is pretty busy now, anyway. The BIA has sent out a man to service the school generator and to check out the water and heating and sewage disposal systems. The project of repainting the school, outside and in, requires extra help from the men of the village. Charlie rounded up his relatives—brothers, nephews, cousins—plus a few other men from the village, and the job will be finished soon.

The women scour the tundra nearly every day, looking for grasses and berries. Mary goes foraging with Liz or Louise to collect salmon berries and blueberries from the low bushes. She carries a little berry basket made for her by her grandmother. She wants to learn how to weave baskets herself, and her grandmother has promised to teach her. Mary enjoys being out with her family, proud of the way her little basket fills up. There is not much temptation to eat the berries rather than to drop them in the basket, because they are very sour. Most of the other children have coffee cans; a few of the women use wooden scoops. When the cans fill up, the children take them to their older relatives and dump them into the bigger containers. At home, they eat the berries fresh in *akutaq* or store them in wooden barrels with seal oil as a preservative or put them in their freezers. Berries are an excellent source of vitamin C, yielding far more of the disease-preventing vitamin than an equal volume of citrus fruits.

No one is idle. Grasses are gathered and dried to make innersoles for mukluks, the sealskin boots. Some women are working on the skins; nearly every house in the village has a couple of sealskins nailed to the wall or the roof. Once the skins are dry, the women scrape off all the hair to make the outer soles of the mukluks. Other women are making nets for the ice fishing that will begin after freeze-up in the fall. Racks of fish, the current catch, dry in the sun.

Before the coming of the white man with his food and goods, the Eskimos were totally dependent on their own resourcefulness in using what the environment offered for everything they needed: homes, clothes, food, tools. But that has changed now, and one of the major events of August is the arrival of the barge, bringing basic supplies for the coming year.

The young boys are the first to spot it, and they run back to the village, shouting. All the able-bodied males are enlisted to help with the unloading, and there is a crowd of spectators to watch the goods come off. An aluminum boat for one of the men in the village. A freezer. A load of lumber for the new generator shed and for replacement of part of the boardwalk. Cartons of merchandise for the two village stores. Cans of motor oil, drums of gasoline.

Liz is watching for the crate that will contain her elegant gold-colored velvet sofa with tufted cushions and a silky fringe around the bottom. It is something she has wanted for a long time, and last winter Charlie told her to go ahead and order it.

In the old days people usually sat on the floor; many women still prefer to sit with their legs stretched straight out in front of them while they sew or work on their skins or baskets. But television, magazines, and mail-order catalogues have also given them gussak ideas of decorating, taking them a long way from the simplicity of the sod house with its minimal furnishings. Preference for sparseness has given way to a taste for ornate carving, fancy fabric, and bric-a-brac. The new sofa will certainly crowd Liz's small living area, and for a long time visitors will probably avoid it because of its awesome newness. But it represents status for Liz: her husband has a job that permits him to buy such things for his family.

For the village as a whole, the most important cargo on the barge from Seattle is the stove oil. Jim had cleaned the thirty drums belonging to his family and rolled them to the unloading area. One by one the empty drums are pumped full and rolled away to be stored. Each family gets its own supply. Everyone has crossed fingers about the oil supply. It always looks huge, and it eats up most of the cash that most of the families have, but if it's an unusually cold winter the residents of the village will begin to worry about using it up before warm weather comes. The barge cannot come when the river is frozen, and the only alternative if the village does run out of fuel before summer is to fly in drums of oil from Outside, an extremely expensive undertaking.

The amount of food ordered by the BIA to feed the two teachers and their family and to operate the school lunch program for an entire year is always an impressive sight. The teachers' big pantry will be completely stocked with all the staples—flour, sugar, rice, coffee—and canned goods that can be consumed in a year. For the school children there are crates of canned beans, tomatoes, fruit juices, lunch meat, macaroni.

And there are all the school supplies, not only paper and pencils and books, but tape cassettes, a new movie projector, new tables and chairs for the first grade room. In a few days the teachers will be coming back from their summer leave, and then the daily routine will begin again. Long days of freedom will be over. Mary is pleased and excited; Andy is not so sure. Pete will not be there this year. He's leaving with Jim for high school in Bethel.

And he is looking forward to it, although he doesn't know much about it. Jim says little about the school and about his life there, and Pete cannot ask him: it would not be proper to question his older brother. One thing he knows is that his mother does not want him to go, but she will not forbid it. There will be three younger children at home, and Andy is already ten—big enough to drive the snow machine to fetch water from the well and do other things to help.

There were seven in Pete's class at the BIA school, and all are going to Bethel except one girl. He is sure that he will stay, even though he guesses he will be homesick long before the Thanksgiving vacation. At least Jim will be in the dorm too, and that will make it easier.

The high school years are hard on parents and on students who leave their families at the age of fourteen to live far from home in a strange place, in a dormitory with students in ninth through twelfth grade who come from more than fifty villages in the region. It's a sharp contrast to the security of home, family, and village.

Before the dorm was built, all students lived in boarding homes with private families who housed and fed the young Eskimos for love or money or other reasons. Sometimes it worked and the host families made the students feel at home; many times there were problems. Now most live in dorms, where, surprisingly, life seems somehow more secure, with its strict set of rules and regulations. But among the students there are tight little cliques from each village and a lot of inter-village rivalry.

The dropout rate is high, especially among the girls, but a few of the students adjust very well. Too well, some believe. Jim's roommate, Paul, says he was not even tempted to come home for seal hunting. It's cold, hard, dangerous work, and there are easier ways to get food.

The night before the students leave for Bethel, the village council sponsors a farewell party for them. Like most farewell parties, there are many mixed emotions. Parents whose children are leaving for the first time are most upset, because they are not sure how the children will react. Maybe they'll change too much and won't want to come home again. Maybe they won't change enough, and they'll be miserable and homesick. It's a good thing, this chance for an education, the parents tell their sons and sometimes their daughters. But inside they're miserable, and the young people are full of anxiety.

The evening begins with a supper in the community hall, a last chance to enjoy native foods before the students go out to gussak cooking. After supper the older folks and young children return home, and an all-night party and dance gets under way for the teen-agers. Somebody hooks up a couple of amplifiers to the stereo system, and rock music blasts across the silent tundra. What we should do the next time, one of the older boys suggests, is to hire the rock band from Shnamute. Everyone laughs, because the musicians are from a Moravian village that prohibits dancing of any kind, even the traditional Eskimo ceremonial dancing. The band can't perform in its own village, but the musicians have been making the rounds of the non-Moravian villages in the area. The boys who have heard them insist that they're very good.

The recorded music goes on without a pause. No one can get any sleep, but there are no complaints: it's for the young people, it's their last night, let them enjoy themselves. Separate groups of boys and girls stand together, lean against the walls, watch the other groups. Not many actually dance. A few couples drift out into the night—darkness comes for a few hours now—and a chance to be alone. Tomorrow means a separation for some of the couples: the boys will be leaving again, but many of the girls will stay at home.

Empty soft drink cans and a few beer cans clatter into cartons. Many of the Bethel students have begun to drink, despite the warnings of their elders. No one is quite sure how the beer got into Chaputnuak, though, given the village ban against any kind of alcohol. It doesn't take much beer to have an effect on the young people, and a few of them are obviously and loudly intoxicated. Some marijuana has been smuggled in, too. Jim was offered joints freely in Anchorage, but he is somewhat surprised to see it in his own village. Most adult Eskimos would swear that none of their young people use drugs of any kind.

By dawn everyone is exhausted. Jim and his friends
—he is still very shy of girls—have decided there is no
point in going to bed now. They go to find something to
eat. Liz is fixing coffee when they come into the house.
She looks very tired and very sad. She makes a shushing
motion; Pete and the young children are still asleep. Jim
smiles; Pete was so sure he'd be able to last the whole night
without sleep.

The Koonuk family is especially sad this time, because
two of its members are going, Jim for his last year, Pete
for his first. Pete is nervous as he packs his clothes after
breakfast. Only a few months ago it seemed this day would
never come. Now that it is here, he is relieved that Jim
will be there to help him get used to all the new things:
people from other villages, a big dormitory, large classes,
different teachers for each course. Jim has told him that it's
good, that the only thing wrong with it, really, is not being
able to come home any time you want to. But Pete has already made up his mind that he will be home for seal hunting next spring.

Late in the morning the plane comes, and the farewells grow more intense. Liz and most of the women are
crying openly. Charlie does not cry, but his face is deeply
furrowed, and he does not look directly at either Jim or
Pete. Liz hugs them both, over and over, reminding them
to take care of themselves, to be good, to study hard, to
come home soon. Charlie shakes hands briefly with each
one, looks away, shoves his hands deep in his pants pockets.
Andy is the brave one, the oldest son at home. In a few

years it will be his turn. Louise holds Mary by the hand; Anna is there with Christine. Grandparents, aunts, uncles look unhappy.

Finally their belongings are loaded, the students are on board, and the plane taxis slowly to the end of the runway. The engine roars; they lift off fast. Everyone on the ground waves, and some wipe their eyes with their sleeves. The plane banks sharply, levels off again, and to those on board the tiny village appears below as a cluster of matchboxes. Jim has an unswallowable lump in his throat. Pete refuses to look back.

September

HAIR NEATLY BRAIDED IN PIGTAILS AND TIED WITH RED yarn, Mary dawdles, giggles, and skips her way to school with her cousin Nancy. Andy and Nancy's brother Jack also walk together, passing a ball back and forth as they go. The girls are second graders this year; Andy is in sixth, and Jack in fifth.

For Andy, not much has changed: same teacher, Mr. McGrath, in the same big room with the fifth through eighth grades. Different books, that's all. Jack has moved over from Mrs. McGrath's second-through-fourth grade room. But for Mary and Nancy, this year is very different. Last year they and the four other first graders had a cozy little room all to themselves, and their own Eskimo teacher, Charlene, taught them reading, printing, arithmetic, science, art, music—everything in Yupik. Once a day Mrs.

McGrath came to teach them English for an hour, using Mother Goose rhymes to get them used to the new language.

Mary has been picking up an English vocabulary for several years. She watches *Sesame Street* regularly on television, and she sometimes hears the older kids speaking English. The Chaputnuak school does not have a kindergarten, although some of the larger villages do. A few years ago a VISTA volunteer had lived in the village for a while. He did not have a formal teaching program, but he spent a lot of time with the children. They were all fond of him and visited him often to play games with him. He spoke English to them; they spoke Yupik to him. Before long the children were using a strange mixture of English words with Eskimo word endings: "chewing gum" for instance, became *gummaq* among the children.

After the VISTA man left, two young women associated with a Catholic missionary organization came to establish a preschool. The village council gave them an old house to live in and helped them fix up the former council store for a schoolroom. The women didn't have much to work with—some broken crayons, rolls of shelf paper, a few ragged books with stories about suburban white children—but they went ahead and tried it anyway. Mary spent a couple of months in the program before she got sick with a chest infection that lasted almost all winter. When their organization ran out of money after two years and the women said they would have to leave, the village council talked about asking them to stay on to keep the

*Children line up
outside the village school.*

preschool running. The council debated for a long time—
hasty decisions are not part of Eskimo culture—before they
came up with an offer. They would provide one of the
women with a place to stay and make sure she had someone
to haul water and pump oil for her. But they didn't think
they could pay her anything, nor could they provide her
with food.

The women considered and said they felt their efforts
were worth *something*. The outspoken member of the team
pointed out that small salaries are available for other town
employees, including the women who call the bingo numbers, so why not for teachers? The council members remained stubbornly unyielding, and the women packed up
and left. The council waited and hoped that another volunteer would appear from somewhere, but none did. So now
the children enter the alien world of the BIA school in first
grade, without any preparation.

At exactly nine o'clock Mrs. McGrath rings the bell,
and the children, who have been standing in the hallway
talking or playing quietly in the classroom, take their assigned seats. It hasn't always worked so smoothly. When
the school was first opened sixteen years ago, and for a long
time after that, the children had a hard time adjusting to
the idea of being in a certain place at a certain time. Eskimos don't operate by the clock, or even by the calendar.
They know by observing signs in nature when it's "time"
for something to be done. The "old teachers," Mr. and
Mrs. Fosdick who were there for seven years before the
McGraths came three years ago, struggled to convince the

students and their parents that it was necessary to be at school at nine o'clock every weekday morning.

When the bell rings, Mary watches a bit wistfully as the first graders follow Charlene into the little room that was converted into a classroom when the bilingual program was begun. It would be nice to be in that room again, she thinks, where there are just a few girls and boys and she could speak Yupik all day long. Instead, she hangs her jacket in the brightly lighted hallway and goes shyly into the classroom for the lower grades.

But like most of the children, Mary really likes being here. Their homes are small, low-ceilinged, dark, cluttered. The classroom is completely different, a level of luxury that the children do not encounter anywhere else in their lives. It's a big, cheerful classroom with carpeting and green chalkboards and bright new furniture. Although the carpet was designed for noise control, it is an unnecessary precaution for Eskimo children. They are used to speaking in low voices, and their behavior is generally quiet and non-aggressive. Across one wall big windows face the western horizon and the village. Many of the children can see their homes from here and can catch glimpses of their parents and other adults out on errands. Planes land and take off at the other end of the village. Snow machines and boats move silently by in their seasons. Chaputnuak is an animated picture framed in the glass windows of the modern gussak school.

Mrs. McGrath has decorated the room with some of the children's art projects, all carefully done from standard patterns and printed sheets. Silhouettes of autumn leaves cut from tissue paper are pasted along the upper glass panels of the windows so the light can shine through. Harvest pictures are spaced along the other walls: armloads of corn, sheafs of wheat, baskets of garden vegetables, cornucopias of peaches, pears, apples. These tie in with a poster near the door showing the different groups of foods that make up a balanced gussak diet: dairy foods, meat and fish, leafy green vegetables, grains, fresh fruits.

The teacher is very fond of plants, and she has arranged over a dozen of them in pots by the window. Most of them sprouted from seeds saved from some of the fresh fruits and vegetables flown in for the McGrath family: a spindly grapefruit tree, a gangling avocado, a trailing squash vine. There are also some cacti from the southwest, and on display, but not sprouting, is a shriveled brown coconut brought by the McGraths from their vacation in Hawaii.

The McGraths are crazy about Hawaii, and every year when they go out on leave they stop over there on the way back from visiting their families in Michigan. They have bought a condominium in Hawaii that they plan to use for their vacations, and they like to tell the children about what they've seen there. The children can find Hawaii on the map. They know of other people who vacation there: Egoak, who owns the village store, has visited there twice, and even Charlie Koonuk has said it's something he'd like to do someday, too.

The first ritual of the morning is the arrival of paper cups of juice carried on trays by two of the children. Vitamin C consumed and empty cups collected, the nineteen pupils in the room line up to repeat the Pledge of Allegiance and to sing "My Country 'Tis of Thee," both in Yupik.

One group settles down with their math workbooks; Sam, the teacher aide, sits with them, quietly answering their questions. At another table, the children fiddle with the dials of an audio-cassette system. Meanwhile, Mrs. McGrath assembles a reading group near the chalkboard. The story they're reading is about a farmer and his wife and their assorted animals. Mrs. McGrath divides the six children into two teams. When she asks a question, a pair of contestants races to the chalkboard to be the first to print the right answer. "What says 'moo' and gives milk?" asks Mrs. McGrath. A boy and girl both manage to write "cow" at the same time, and each receives a point. Neither has ever seen a cow—or a chicken, pig, sheep, horse, or turkey that make up the rest of the lesson. "At Thanksgiving," Mrs. McGrath asks next, "what will we all have to eat?" "Turkey," they write, in variant spellings.

The morning goes by in a busy hum. Before recess, Mrs. McGrath passes out ditto sheets with pictures of different kinds of trees to color and tells them to do their best, because some of the pictures will be mounted on the display board out in the hall. The children of the treeless tundra are careful to stay inside the faint bluish lines. When they finish, the aide puts on his jacket and motions them outside. The rain has stopped although it is still very windy. "Exercises!" he calls. Some of the children line up in front of a boy who has appointed himself their leader. Counting loudly in English, the children follow their

leader through a series of windmills and jumping jacks before they scatter to run races or play ball.

When Mary finishes her arithmetic with a little sur-
reptitious help from Nancy (white teachers still struggle
against this kind of cooperation that is taken for granted
among Eskimo children), Mrs. McGrath tells her that she
may do whatever she wants until lunchtime. Mary pulls a
picture book from the shelf. She doesn't bother with the
words, but she likes to turn the pages and look at the bright
pictures. The story is about a black child who wanders
through a department store looking for a teddy bear. Mary
has never seen a black child, except on television. She has
never been in a department store. And she has never had a
teddy bear or any other kind of stuffed animal. Mary turns
the pages slowly, gazing at the pictures absent-mindedly,
until the lunch bell rings.

The children march in pairs down the polished corridor to pick up their lunch trays from the kitchen. Old
Mrs. Erickson scoops the food onto paper plates: chicken-
noodle casserole, canned spinach, canned tomatoes, crackers, chocolate pudding, milk. Mary carefully carries her
tray back to her seat. When everyone has been served, Mrs.
McGrath gives her lesson in manners: how to unfold the
paper napkin and place it on the lap, how to hold the fork
and spoon. When there is lunch meat, she teaches them
how to hold the fork in one hand and the knife in the
other for cutting—all gussak etiquette, of course, not Eskimo.

Mary picks dutifully at the food. The spinach does

not taste at all like the wild greens her mother serves in early summer with salt and sea oil. She pokes the tomato experimentally and tastes some of the chicken-noodle dish. It's better than the vegetables, and she eats a little of it. Then she drinks all of her milk and finishes the pudding in no time.

Some of the children eat most of the food served, but generally the younger ones leave more than half the lunch on their plates. When the "old teachers" were here, Andy told Mary, everybody had to eat everything on the plate. The children didn't like the gussak food, and some of them got sick on it. One day a delegation of parents had gone to school to speak to the teachers about it. In those days almost everyone was afraid to say anything: they didn't want to seem ungrateful by criticizing the white teachers' efforts. Wouldn't it be possible, they found courage to ask, to give the children the kind of food they were used to? Dried fish and seal meat?

Certainly, the Fosdicks had replied, if the people of the village were willing to provide it. But if they were not, then the children must eat the food that is provided by the government. It is the children's duty to eat every bite, they said, and to be grateful for it.

Mr. and Mrs. McGrath have a different philosophy. They encourage the children to eat the gussak food, but they don't force them. As a result, some of the children go home hungry. No longer so reticent as they once were, the parents have recently complained that their children are not getting enough to eat. Mr. McGrath showed the parents the quantities of food being left on the children's plates, and he explained to them that only enough food has been ordered to last for one school year. If they serve more food each day, it will simply be wasted; the children will not eat it, and there will not be enough in the spring. The parents went away dissatisfied, but they don't know how they can persuade the United States government to feed Eskimo children with Eskimo food.

After lunch most of the children go outside again, but in the upper-class room a few students stay inside to relax. Andy challenges a friend to Chinese checkers; two girls have a game of ringtoss. One student is making more figures for the model of an Eskimo village spread out on a table near the window. The little houses are built of construction paper, arranged around a pond and a river. The figures in the village, as well as seals and a few boats, have been carefully fashioned of clay, and the student is struggling to model a miniature snow machine. In the middle of the village is a small printed sign mounted on a toothpick: *Keep America Beautiful.*

In this more formally structured classroom students sit in straight rows of desk-seat units facing the front of the room. Mr. McGrath, an easy-going man in jeans and a plaid shirt, calls his eighth-grade reading group to a corner by the chalkboard and introduces them to a humorous story about a family that goes trout fishing in Yellowstone National Park. He patiently explains where Yellowstone is, and how trout fishing differs from ice fishing and salmon fishing. Early in the story the family's dog encounters one of the Yellowstone bears who toys with it, tossing it into the air "like a shuttlecock." Mr. McGrath draws a deep breath and describes a shuttlecock, sketching it on the chalkboard. Then he compares the game of badminton to tennis, which his students have seen on television. By the time he has finished translating the metaphor, the thread of the story is weakened and the humor of the incident is lost forever. In the next paragraph he has to start all over with a definition of "pirouette."

Before the group breaks up, Mr. McGrath mentions casually to them, and to the others in the room, that his younger brother is coming to visit sometime during the winter. He has never been to Alaska, and he is coming all the way from New York. "How many know where New York is?" No hands. Mr. McGrath calls on one of the girls. "Anchorage?" she offers tentatively. "No, but has anyone else an idea?" "Italy," suggests one of the boys. Mr. Mc-Grath pulls down a map to cover the chalkboard and points out New York, showing them how his brother will fly to Chicago and then make an arc up over Canada to reach Anchorage, then Bethel, then Chaputnuak. Thirty-five hundred miles, he tells them. Andy starts daydreaming about Anchorage, and how he's going to go there some day the way his brother Jim did. There are no questions about the unknown New York.

Later in the afternoon one of the men in the village comes to the school to sing Eskimo songs for the children. Mr. McGrath takes his students to the other classroom, where the tables and chairs have been pushed aside and everyone sits on the floor. The children all know Tony and have heard his songs often, but they love to have him come. Many years ago they would have learned these ancient songs in the *qasegiq,* but now they hear them only at the winter potlatches, and when Tony comes to school.

Mrs. McGrath has her Polaroid camera ready, and she takes his picture and pastes it in the school guest book. She does not embarrass him by asking him to sign his name but prints it under his picture with the date. Sometimes the children like to turn the pages to see who some of the other visitors have been: the visiting doctor and dentist, the lady from the television station in Bethel, the men who installed the big metal "saucer" for the earth station, part of the new telephone system that will make it possible to call distant places. The radio men stayed with one of the families in the village, and once they came to Mary's house to speak to her father. Her mother invited them to have tea. Mary watched silently, but her brother Andy went right up to them and began to ask questions about what they were doing. When they saw her later in the classroom, one said, "Hi, Mary," and made her blush.

When Mary was in first grade, their teacher had helped them to make a book of their own. Charlene came to their homes with that Polaroid camera and took pictures of them getting ready for school. Some of the pictures showed her classmates eating breakfast or brushing their teeth. Charlene snapped two pictures of Mary putting on her parka. The first one showed it laid on the floor as she crawled in; in the second shot she was standing up, flipping it over her head and arms, the way all the children do it.

Charlene let them handle the camera themselves, when she was sure they'd be careful, and they photographed the things they did all day in school: eating lunch, writing on the board, coloring pictures. When all the photographs had been pasted on cardboard pages and tied together with yarn, Mrs. McGrath printed captions for each picture in English and Charlene printed them in Yupik.

After school Mary and Nancy decide to visit Mrs. McGrath and her little boy, Teddy. The McGraths always stay in the school building until five o'clock, since they are required as employees of the government to put in an eight-hour day. The girls play on the seesaws and jungle gym until they see Mrs. McGrath cross the boardwalk that connects the school to the living quarters. The girls think Mrs. McGrath is beautiful. She wears pantsuits like the ones in the catalogue, and her hair is done up like a TV star's. She always looks as though she is dressed up to go somewhere, even when she is at home. The McGraths don't do much visiting around the village, although Mr. McGrath sometimes goes out fox hunting with the men. But Mrs. McGrath likes to have the women visit her occasionally, and she shows them the beautiful embroidery work she does as a hobby. The children are welcome to stop in for short visits, as long as there aren't too many at one time, and as long as Teddy isn't sleeping.

When the girls come shyly to the door of the teacher's quarters, it is Nancy's mother who lets them in. She sometimes babysits while Mrs. McGrath is teaching. When she can't come, Nancy's grandmother takes over, or one of the other relatives. Caring for little blue-eyed blond-haired Edward McGrath is a sort of family project.

The house itself is as much of an attraction for the children as the baby is. First Mary pauses to admire the kitchen: flowered wallpaper, shiny stove and refrigerator, and best of all, a sink with hot and cold running water. There's a separate laundry room with a washer and dryer, and next to that is the pantry with the whole year's food supply for the family stored in orderly rows, better than the village store. When she has examined it all, Mary tip-toes into the living room. The couch matches the two up-holstered chairs, and tables with lamps stand beside each one. There's a low table in front of the sofa and another big wooden one with chairs at one end of the living room, in addition to the dinette set in the kitchen. The stereo set and a television are built into a polished cabinet with fancy doors.

Mr. and Mrs. McGrath sleep in a bedroom all by themselves. The baby and the little girl, Carole, share the other bedroom. The first time she came to visit, Mary asked why the children didn't sleep in the same big bed with the parents. None of the babies she knows have fenced- in beds like Teddy's crib. Mrs. McGrath explained that many people on the Outside believe it's healthier for a baby to have his own bed and even his own room, and that it's better for the parents, too. Mary is not sure about that. Evon sleeps with her mother and father: he would be very lonely if he didn't, Mary thinks, and Teddy must not really like it this way.

Nancy's mother says all the beautiful furniture does

not really belong to the McGraths; it is the property of the BIA. Mrs. McGrath has told her that they stored all their own furniture somewhere Outside, and that when they go back to Michigan to live they will be happy to have their own things again.

The most fascinating room in the house for all the visiting Eskimo children is the bathroom. The bathtub and shower actually work, and there's an electrically-operated chemical toilet. Mary always make it a point to use the bathroom when she comes to visit, to try out the toilet— she pushes a button and there's a humming sound that frightened her at first, and blue liquid squirts in and washes everything away—and to weigh herself on the bathroom scales.

The women of the village are more interested in the automatic clothes dryer. Most of the men and some of the women have discovered that down-filled parkas ordered from the catalogue are warm enough for all but the coldest weather and are much lighter than the traditional skin parkas. They can be washed all right, but they must be fluff-dried in an automatic dryer, rather than hung on a clothesline, to keep the down filling from matting. And so Mrs. McGrath allows them to bring their parkas to her dryer, a much different attitude than the Fosdicks, who never let anybody use anything, claiming that it cost the government too much money.

The McGraths are well-liked in Chaputnuak, because they seem to like the village and its people. Steve McGrath, who grew up in northern Michigan, is an avid snowmo-

biler and hunter. He admires the Eskimos for their practical wisdom, their sense of the balance of nature, their
simplicity and open honesty. He hopes they don't lose
their good qualities as they acquire some of the gussak
values in which he is trying to educate them.

Ginny McGrath has adapted less easily than her husband. When she first came to Alaska to teach, she had all
sorts of ideas of how she was going to help the Eskimos improve their lot. She was going to teach them about nutri-
tion, showing them ways of cooking good, inexpensive
foods. She was going to teach them about hygiene. She
was planning to work with the girls to show them how to
be good household managers and budget-keepers. But she
has not been able to accomplish any of these things. The
women are all very polite and kind, but they seem unwill-
ing to become involved in any of her projects. Furthermore,
she finds them unreliable. The babysitters all know what
time she must be at school each morning, yet she is never
quite sure who is coming to stay with Teddy, or what time
the sitter will arrive. But she is a great admirer of native
crafts, and in her three years in Chaputnuak she has as-
sembled an extensive collection of ivory jewelry, baskets,
two fur parkas, and several pairs of mukluks for themselves and relatives on the Outside. Both McGraths have
taken lots of photographs of birds, flowers, and people.

At the end of this year they will leave, believing that
four years is long enough in one village. From Chaputnuak
they will go to a larger school in the interior, where the students will be Athabascan Indians, rather than Eskimos,

and Steve will be principal with a staff of five teachers and several teacher aides. After that contract is up, they'll go Outside again. They will have had their Alaskan adventure and saved up some money. Their present salaries are much higher than anything they will be able to earn in schools in the Lower Forty-Eight, and since the BIA rents them furnished quarters at modest rates and there are none of the other major expenses of living Outside—a car, for instance—they have been able to set aside quite a lot of money, part of which they invested in their Hawaiian condominium.

The cost of running the BIA school in Chaputnuak is enormous, far more than for any school on the Outside. The equipment—more than they can use—is the most up-to-date, some of it more expensive than most Outside school districts could hope to afford. The McGraths are experienced, competent teachers. The children are polite and cooperative; none of that aggressive behavior that often causes problems in many Outside schools. And yet the McGraths see the children falling farther and farther behind.

Once a month or so Steve and Ginny go to visit the teachers in one of the other villages, or somebody comes to visit them. They have known most of the BIA teachers for several years, and they have a pleasant social life with them. Invariably, the talk gets around to the problems of Eskimo education. Some of the teachers frankly admit that they believe the Eskimos are *nice* folks but not quite bright; it's a waste of government funds to be trying to train them for the white world, when they just don't have the mentality to absorb it. Other teachers—the young, idealistic ones—feel that the Eskimos, like the American Indians, have been treated harshly by the white man, that their lands have been taken away and their culture virtually destroyed. They accept it as a personal challenge to try to make amends by educating their Eskimo students. The Eskimos resent the first viewpoint and are wary of the second. But nobody—not even the Eskimos—is quite sure what "educating" Eskimos really means. Is it helping them to become better Eskimos? Or to make them more like gussaks? But the Eskimos agree on one thing: when they control their own education, they will also control their own destiny.

Eskimo education, whether administered by the Bureau of Indian Affairs, the missionary societies, or the state of Alaska, has always been in the hands of white men, but that is now changing. Chaputnuak is perhaps typical of what has been happening in Eskimo villages throughout Alaska: the teachers are professional and sympathetic; the facilities are superior; but the subject matter and the techniques for transmitting it have been strictly the white man's idea of how Eskimos should be educated, and the results are dismal. Even as Alaskan natives assume control of their schools and establish new goals, it will take a long time to change direction. Steve and Ginny McGrath wait to see what will happen. Meanwhile, they do the best they can.

Part 2

FREEZE-UP

JACKET COLLAR TURNED UP AGAINST THE SHARP NORTH wind, hands jammed in his jeans pockets, Pete Koonuk strolls along the banks of the Kuskokwim where it loops around Bethel. For the past few days the puddles of rainwater collected outside the student dormitory have had a thin skin of ice. This morning the skin had turned solid, all the way through. And so when classes were over, Pete walked through town to the river. Sure enough, the edges of the dark water were iced with white. If the cold weather holds, the river will be solidly frozen in another couple of weeks.

Freeze-up is inevitable, but more subtle than the dramatic moment of breakup. Once breakup occurs, there's no turning back: the process—from that first grinding of the winter ice, until the last floe moves out into the Bering Sea

—is inexorable. Freeze-up isn't like that. A warm spell could sweep up from the south, and the ice would fade away. Everybody is ready for it, though, when it comes. Dozens of bright-colored planes tied up along the river bank have been switched from floats to skis. Frozen ponds and rivers will shorten the distance between two points. Snow machines will roar; people will start traveling again.

Pete looks at the river and thinks about home. Everything he sees and hears reminds him of home. Pete is miserable. He had not expected the homesickness to be so bad.

The high school is much bigger than he had imagined, even though Jim had told him a little about it. The teachers are really nice—particularly the math teacher, who has told Pete that he has real talent if he'll stick with it. The dormitory is pleasant, and Mr. Frederickson, the director, does everything he can to help. Even the food is pretty good, especially the breakfasts. Eggs every morning, if you want them. Pancakes and sausages on Sunday. But no smoked fish, no seal oil, no *akutaq*.

And the dorm is nothing like home. Pete has not discussed his feelings with anyone, and he has no way of knowing if anybody else has experienced this same peculiar sensation in the pit of the stomach. He would not say anything to Jim about it, and Jim would not say anything to him. But his brother has suggested, the first week they were here, that the church parish house was a good place to go when classes were over and there wasn't much else to do.

So Pete has become a regular at the church, mostly

playing Ping-Pong, or just sitting around reading comic books or talking, sometimes to Father Bob, the priest. Pete and Jim go to mass every Sunday, just as they did at home, and sometimes Pete goes during the week, too. Before they left Chaputnuak, there had been a special sermon for the departing students, admonishing them to remain faithful churchgoers and good Catholics. And most of them have, because it seems one comforting link with home.

Home. If he were home now, Pete would be out testing the ice on the pond, and he'd have his skates sharpened and ready for the first day it would hold him. For the first couple of weeks after freeze-up, the pond would be the center of attraction for village kids and some of the grown-ups, too. Then the snow would come and cover the ice, and that would be the end of the brief skating season.

Home. If he were home now, he would be getting ready for ice fishing, and maybe helping his father to tinker with the snow machine. They'd be talking about trapping. He'd be eating smoked salmon and playing with Mary and Evon and moving his sleeping bag closer to the stove—he still hasn't gotten used to the dormitory bunkbeds.

Home. He won't be there until Thanksgiving, a long time from now. He wonders if his family misses him as much as he misses them. He is sure they do, and knowing it makes him feel better. On the way back to the dorm he stops off at the parish house to challenge Father Bob to a game of Ping-Pong and beats him handily.

October

ANNA SUCKS THE COLD AIR INTO HER LUNGS AND PICKS OUT the figure of her brother Andy skimming along over the frozen pond, his skates flashing as he races three of his friends. Off to one side the girls skate sedately, holding hands and chattering. Near the edge the younger ones—Mary is among them—take tentative little shuffles, fall down, scramble up again, shuffle a few more steps.

Anna watches them, baby Christine snug against her hip, remembering when she was young and skated every chance she could—at night by moonlight was the best—during that short period between freeze-up and the first heavy snow. Last year she was pregnant with Christine. This year she is pregnant again. Even if she were not, there would be no skating for Anna and probably won't be ever again. Mothers of young children are criticized if they do anything so frivolous as skating; they should be at home with the babies. And by the time the last baby is old enough to be out skating too, the women are no longer much interested in skating themselves.

The baby was conceived, Anna believes, before Carl left for work at the cannery. She has not yet told him, because she knows that once *he* knows, she will have to listen just that much longer to his insistence that the baby must be a boy. And she has not yet said anything to her mother, but she decides she must ask somebody soon if there's anything she can do to make sure this baby is a boy.

Anna is on her way home from the health clinic, where she picked up some cough medicine for Christine. Years ago—and today in a few of the less progressive villages—the clinic was part of the school and the BIA teacher had health care among his many responsibilities. But the old system has been generally phased out. The Chaputnuak clinic occupies two small rooms in the community center, staffed by two young Eskimo women, Nina and Marie, high school graduates who have taken the short, intensive course for health aides and who are called in periodically for additional training. They dispense common medicines—antibiotics, aspirin, some pain relievers—and they give the children their inoculations, but their main diagnostic and treatment tool is the radio that keeps them in touch with doctors at the Public Health Service hospital in Bethel.

When Anna got the cough medicine, she mentioned to Nina in a rather off-hand way that she believes she is pregnant again. Nina promptly went into action. She took Anna's blood pressure, tested her urine, helped her figure

out when the baby is due, weighed her and reminded her
not to gain too much. She also gave her a bottle of vitamin
pills and another of iron tablets. No advice on sex deter-
mination, but she promised not to say anything to Carl.

When the public health nurse comes around again,
she will examine Anna thoroughly. But as long as Anna is
feeling well, there is no need to go to Bethel until near time
for delivery. Then she will check into the Bethel pre-
maternal home to wait until labor begins. A few years ago
most women had their babies at home; today most arrange
to go to the PHS hospital.

The younger people in the village take the PHS hospital for granted, even though it is an old building and
understaffed, with only fifty beds and seven doctors to
serve more than fifteen thousand people spread out over a
huge area. The older people, fearing the journey and the
unfamiliarity, still sometimes fall back on their old ways.
Andy remembers when he broke his arm last year and his
grandmother tied a piece of red yarn near the break, before
the plane took him to the hospital for emergency treatment. Andy remembers his embarrassment when the young
doctor cut the yarn away, laughing and shaking his head.
"Someday," Andy heard the doctor telling the nurse who
assisted him, "I'm going to write a book about some of these
crazy folk remedies."

Andy did not tell that doctor about the time his father
had hurt his back and one of the old men of the village had
treated the injury with an "Eskimo shot" that resembles
acupuncture. Andy had watched silently while the old
man seized a pinch of flesh in his father's strong-muscled

back and squeezed it hard to deaden the pain. Then he had taken a very thin, sharp hacksaw blade and run it quickly in and out of the fold of flesh. There was a little bleeding, but his father had not even gasped. A few minutes later his father stood up, flexed his shoulders and stretched his back, and announced that the pain was already less. By the next day, it was entirely gone.

Health care is a huge problem in such a remote area. There are no doctors in the villages to deal with emergencies. If the weather is good and Bethel has a plane available, it still takes an hour for the plane to reach the village to pick up the patient, another hour to fly back. But coastal weather is fickle, and it's often days before a plane can get in. Villagers of Chaputnuak carry the grim memory of a young man who developed acute appendicitis during a winter storm. There were no planes for a week, and the appendix ruptured. The health aides did what little they could, and the priest said prayers, but the patient died before the weather lifted.

Visiting nurses come every month or so, sometimes spotting problems that need more help. Once or twice a year doctors from Bethel and Anchorage make their rounds, giving everyone in the village a thorough checkup. But routine health care in village Alaska depends on the astuteness of the health aides at the clinic. This might be adequate for a generally healthy population. Unfortunately, Eskimos are especially vulnerable to respiratory diseases, such as tuberculosis, influenza, and pneumonia. Everyone in the village is tested regularly for TB. A few years ago, the rate of tuberculosis among Alaskan natives, Eskimos and Indians, was estimated at *twenty times* the rate for the United States as a whole. And infant mortality, with pneumonia as the principal cause of death, was about seven times the infant mortality for the U.S. in general.

There are a number of reasons for these frightening statistics. One is that the Eskimos apparently do have inherent respiratory weakness. When the white man arrived, bringing with him the germs that cause these respiratory illnesses, the Alaskan natives were not physically able to combat the infection.

This weakness is complicated by the unsanitary conditions that exist in most of the villages. In Chaputnuak the sewage from the honeybuckets is dumped on the river ice, which is carried out to sea in the spring, but not all villages are located near fast-moving water that removes the accumulated waste. In some places the sewage is dumped on the tundra outside the village. In spring the disease germs also thaw, and epidemics are as inevitable as breakup. None of the villages has a system of running water for drinking and washing; water comes from wells or is hauled from nearby lakes, and this water is often contaminated. Another factor is the location of many villages in low, marshy areas that are often flooded in the spring, when refuse and vermin are swept in with the high water. It's not surprising under the circumstances that the life span of Alaskan natives is much shorter than that of Alaskan whites.

In the afternoon when school is out, Mary stops to see her mother's mother, Amelia. One of the best basketmakers in the village, Amelia is teaching Mary the first steps of her craft: *mingqaaliyaraq*. Together they sit on the floor, their feet stuck out in front of them. Mary clutches a bundle of grasses and tries hard to imitate each step precisely. Between them is a pile of dried grass wrapped in an old cloth. Last spring Amelia had gathered clumps of winter-stained, wrinkled grass—only wild rye grass is flexible enough for basketry—to form the center core of the coil. Then soon after the first frost, Amelia and Mary had picked new grass, blade by blade, allowed it to dry and cure, and stripped off and discarded the mid-rib of each blade.

Most of the grasses are nearly white, but some of them have been dyed rich colors. Grandmother still takes the trouble to make her own dyes, obtaining colors from onion skins, iris petals, beets, coffee grounds, stinkweed, blueberries, and such non-organic sources as crepe paper, new sweatshirts, and even Hershey bar wrappers.

Amelia knots together the ends of several strands of winter grass for the core. Then she threads a single blade of white or colored grass through a big-eyed needle. She sucks on the blade a little to soften and shape it and begins to wrap it around and around the bundle of winter grass, stitching it over and over, working in more strands to keep the core smooth. It's a sewing process, not weaving like the baskets in other parts of Alaska.

Mary has already learned to make the flat coil that forms the bottom of the basket. Next her grandmother shows her how to build up the sides, flaring them out, to make a shallow saucer-shaped basket. Mary will need much practice to learn how to bring in the sides again slowly, tapering toward the opening at the top, and how to work in the design of red and green birds that march in rows around the basket. The last thing she will do is form the fitted lid.

Amelia's baskets are graceful as sculptured vases, but Mary is already finding that hers is growing a bit lopsided. The old woman talks to her quietly while they work, advising on how to keep the shape of the basket even, telling her stories between bits of advice.

Now that the weather is cold again, Amelia works a few hours each day on her baskets. As she finishes one every ten days or two weeks, she packs it carefully in a cardboard box and mails it to a man in Anchorage who says he will buy everything she makes. He pays her fifty dollars for the small baskets without lids, eighty for the big, lidded ones. She knows he sells them for much more than that, but she does not mind very much.

Another major craft, ivory carving, is no longer so important in Chaputnuak as it once was. Ivory from the gigantic tusks of the walrus is scarce here, and few men remember how to work with it. In some villages it disappeared completely when the Moravian missionaries discouraged such image-making. Once a year Paul Kasak, a man from a village to the north, comes to the school to demonstrate ivory carving. He arrives on his snow machine, carrying a handsome attache case with his tools and a few samples of his work. His specialty is lifelike carvings of birds of the tundra, a technique he has learned from his father and his grandfather.

Paul spreads newspapers out on the schoolroom floor, and after he has passed around his tools and explained what each is for, he invites the children to try working on bars of soap. Using a small paring knife, he shows them how they can make a little boat. Last year when he visited, Andy had been talked into trying it. He had hung back at first until Mr. McGrath singled him out. "Andy here is a real good carver," he said. And then there wasn't any way for Andy to get out of it.

Andy didn't think he was real good at all, but he huddled over his work so that the others couldn't see what he was doing until he had finished. The soap was soft and easy to work with, and in a few minutes he had fashioned a bird that looked a lot like the ptarmigan he had intended. Paul asked him if he minded showing what he had made. Reluctantly Andy handed him the small carved figure. Paul smiled and passed it around. Everyone agreed that it was good. Paul told him, speaking in English, "You have real talent. Keep at it, and someday you may be a first-rate carver."

Andy had blushed and stuffed the soap-bird into his pocket. It was fun to do, but he wasn't sure that he wanted to spend his life making little figures.

After she puts away the beginnings of her small basket, Mary goes home to play with little Evon. Her mother is busy working on a new pair of mukluks for her father. "Mukluk" means "large seal" in Eskimo and has become

the white man's word for the sealskin boot; Eskimos call
them by a variety of other names, depending on the style
and function.

Liz is constructing the mukluks to stop just below the
knee, with a cloth cuff and drawstring around the top to
keep out the snow and cold air, and thongs that cross over
the foot and wrap around the ankle. They are to be plain,
serviceable boots without the fancy work that she sometimes does on the boots ordered by the McGraths and
other gussaks. She cuts the skins by eye, pleats the toe of
the hairless bottom sole with tiny crimps after chewing the
skin to make it pliable, and sews it to the rough-haired
uppers with tiny, even stitches, her needle threaded with
dental floss.

In the past it was the work of every Eskimo woman
to do all the skin sewing for her family. Besides mukluks,
each member of the family had to have at least one fur
parka, the fur on the inside for warmth, the carefully fitted
hood edged with a ruff of wolverine. Today, however, she
does much less skin sewing than she once did. The children
prefer gussak clothing; so, often, do their parents. But most
of the old people say that when it's really cold, there's nothing like fur for warmth.

Mr. McGrath has asked Liz to make a pair of mukluks
for his brother who is coming to visit. For that special pair
she will make inlays of black and white calfskin and add a
strip of mink around the top with perhaps a set of wolverine
tassels.

Mrs. McGrath has ordered some beadwork necklaces
from Frances Koonuk. Like basketry, beadwork is a com-

paratively new craft among Eskimos who have been encouraged by the white man to develop "traditional" crafts. Russian traders brought beads, which the Eskimos used two centuries ago to make elaborate dangling earrings and labrets (worn through the lower lip) for both men and women. Frances never wore a labret, but she did have her septum pierced, a small hole made in the center membrane of her nose, so that she could wear nose beads. The hole is still there, and sometimes to amuse her grandchildren she draws a sewing needle through the tiny opening. Of course no one makes labrets or nose beads these days, but Frances makes elaborate necklaces, using traditional designs that she learned as a child.

Louise is learning beadwork from this grandmother. She has a small loom that Charlie made for her, and she is able to weave a pattern of tiny, bright-colored beads into simple necklaces for herself and her friends—a flat strap that goes around the neck and joins in the front with a sort of medallion and lots of beads dangling from it. Louise likes to experiment, making up new designs as she goes along. Sometimes she even earns a little money selling them.

The days are shorter now, and the village begins its final preparations for winter. Charlie nails a plywood skirting around the stilts of his house in an attempt to reduce the drafts that will sweep up through the floor, chilling his home in the cold days and increasing the consumption of stove oil.

Before the ice gets too thick, Andy helps him put their blackfish trap out in the river. Their funnel-shaped trap is woven with strips of driftwood, and they set it under the ice with a marker that will show them where it is even after deep snow has fallen. Every few days they open the hole in the ice over it, lift out the trap, and empty the fish into a sack. When they release the trap, they put some of the chipped ice back in the hole. In a few hours it is completely frozen over again; when they return in a few days to check it again, there may be a foot of snow to dig through, and certainly more ice to chip away to reach the trap. Through October and November, while the blackfish are running, Liz will serve them boiled, but some will be frozen to eat later, dipped raw in seal oil.

Cold weather alters social life, too. One of the big events at the start of winter is the school Halloween party for the children and their families. Although Andy believes he might be too old for such things, Mary is excited about the party. Charlie bought her a rubber mask, the face of a gnarled old white woman with a big hooked nose, warts, fierce chin, and wisps of gray hair stitched across the forehead. Mary wears one of Liz's old *qaspeqs,* a scarf tied over her head, and a blanket clutched around her shoulders, and she practices a bent-over kind of hobble. Andy decides finally that he will disguise himself as a ferocious animal. He has Pete's old wolf mask, and he plans to wear his parka turned fur side out.

On the night of the party, the whole Koonuk family goes to school. The adults sit awkwardly in a circle of undersized chairs with Evon wide-eyed on Charlie's lap. The children carry their costumes under their arms in bundles and rush into the rest rooms to put them on. Three men from the village council act as judges, and after much careful deliberation they pick the three best costumes from each grade. Each winner—an aged crone with warts is one of them—gets a bag of candy treats before unmasking.

A half-dozen adults have also come in costume. There is much laughter and guessing at the identities, and no one is really surprised when the masks come off. The judges solemnly award three more bags of candy.

After the costume judging, the McGraths organize the games: musical chairs, stomping on balloons, a race pushing a peanut the length of the schoolroom with one's nose. Finally they pass around some gussak food: canned Spam sandwiches on white bread, glasses of Kool-Aid, and cookies. The party is over. Louise offers to take Mary around the village for trick-or-treat, and within an hour they've collected a sack of treats that includes tea bags, packets of soup, a new toothbrush, and enough candy for a week of stomachaches.

Although the Eskimos are sociable people and enjoy visiting back and forth, there are not many community events like this one. When Tom, the VISTA volunteer, was in town he had tried to organize some social life for the young people, who seemed at loose ends with the usual complaints of nothing to do and no place to go. Tom had asked the Fosdicks to let him use one of the schoolrooms for Friday night dances, and when they refused he convinced the council to let him use an empty store that later became the preschool. Tom played the guitar, and he taught one of the boys to play the harmonica. Between the two of them they were able to produce some danceable music, and for a few Friday nights everyone in the village turned out to learn what Tom called square dancing. It was rare for some of the young husbands and wives to socialize together, rarer still for them to dance. Then some faint muttering from the old people grew increasing audible: young couples should be at home with their children, not out behaving like children themselves. Eventually the popularity of the dances declined, and finally they died out altogether.

After the community center was built, the preschool volunteers who came after the VISTA man got the idea of organizing a social club for the teen-agers. They borrowed a record player and bought some games, and every Friday night they hung out a sign that said Tundra Club. It was a popular notion from the start; too popular. The murmurings of the old folks grew into a loud complaint that included the voices of the parents. Exactly what was going on at the Tundra Club, they wanted to know. Boys and girls should be at home with their families in the evenings, not hanging out together and thinking up who-knows-what bad sort of activities. And so the Tundra Club folded, too. Now there's no entertainment for the young people of the village, a situation especially hard on those like Louise who have dropped out of school and have nothing to do but wonder where their lives are headed.

The curfew for school children, sometimes enforced but often ignored, is nine o'clock, and by then most of the kids have drifted toward their homes. The moon, scarcely noticed in the sunlit summer, glows brilliantly in the sky. A jet bound for Tokyo blinks among the stars.

November

Mary has cut out the silhouette of a turkey gob-
bler, which joins a frieze of identical turkeys along the top
of one of the chalkboards. She has also colored a ditto sheet
of a Pilgrim boy in a tall hat and buckled shoes and a girl
in a long dress and apron, giving both of them yellow hair
and blue eyes. Mrs. McGrath has read them all the story
of the First Thanksgiving, and the school kitchen has produced a complete dinner of roast turkey sent by the BIA,
instant mashed potatoes, canned cranberry sauce, canned
corn, and pumpkin pie. Their minds are not on the meaning of the holiday, or even on the food; everybody is watching the airstrip for the plane with their older brothers and
sisters, coming home from Bethel for their first visit since
August.

Egoak ordered thirty frozen turkeys, and every one of
them has been sold. On Thanksgiving Day there is turkey

on nearly every table in the village, not stuffed and roasted but served Eskimo style: boiled with rice and onions. Koonuks, of course, have a big one. While he enjoys the giblets, the real delicacies always saved for the head of the house, Charlie tells Jim and Pete that he has gotten the chicken wire they need to make the mink traps. This is the beginning of the trapping season, and while the boys are home they will bury the cone-shaped traps under the snow near the frozen streams to catch the mink that feed in the water under the ice. Mink skins, dark and glossy with a little white patch at the throat, are the most valuable, but sometimes they get muskrat and otter in their traps, too.

Fur has been one of the chief sources of cash for Eskimo families. At times many Eskimos became so dependent on furs for trading and for cash that they stopped hunting for food. Then when there was a scarcity of certain fur animals, or when the fashion for certain types of fur disappeared and demand declined, they suffered greatly.

Fur trapping today is chiefly the domain of the younger men. Charlie doesn't do much trapping any more, although before he got the school job he was considered one of the best trappers in the village. The Koonuk family once had extensive trap lines—not a "line" at all but an area that was recognized by other families as theirs for trapping, passed down through the generations. Charlie had fifty traps then, and he was often away for days at a time, traveling far from the village to check on them.

It was Liz's job to skin out the animals he brought home, a dirty and unpleasant job. She deftly cut away the

*Ice floes move downriver
past a Russian Orthodox church.*

sac under the tail that produced the acrid odor, cleaned the skins, and turned them inside out to dry, with a board inserted and hung on a clothesline somewhere in the house. Then Charlie would take the furs to Bethel, where they command good prices. For years that had been their winter source of income. But now that Charlie has the school job, he keeps only a few traps close to the village.

One day during the Thanksgiving vacation, Jim and his friends borrow their fathers' snow machines and ride out over the tundra toward the sea. Along the way they spot an Arctic fox, now turned pure white and nearly invisible against the ice and snow. Jim and his friends chase it down, running it back and forth. The fox is quick and wiley, but eventually it drops from exhaustion. Jim reaches it first and hits it over the head with a hammer. Before they return home they catch another one. Each is tied on the back of a snow machine. The pelts are valuable and will fetch perhaps $150 apiece from the dealer in Bethel.

Jim remembers the year before he went to Bethel when one of the men shot a wolverine, and everyone in the village had run to see it. It looked a little like a small bear with a magnificently bushy tail. Wolverine is scarce here; like the polar bear it needs hills and trees, and the tundra is too open and flat for it to hide. The men had known it was around, though, because it had been robbing their traps, both of bait and of small animals. Then one day they saw it, and every man in the village ran for his gun. There was much congratulation of the one who shot it. The fur is highly prized for trim for parka hoods and cuffs, because

*Patience and skill
at "hooking" may yield
a sack of fish.*

the fur does not hold moisture and is therefore frostproof.

On his way home, Jim notices that his father's snow machine is not running as smoothly as it should. His father comes out of the house to meet him; he could tell from the sound as Jim roared across the frozen pond that something was not quite right. Gloveless, Charlie begins to work on it, removing, cleaning, replacing, adjusting, trying again. Eskimos' reputation for mechanical ingenuity is well deserved in Charlie's case. He keeps his own machine in perfect condition, and he is often called to look at another that someone regards as nearly hopeless. Jim watches him closely, wishing he had that talent.

One of the old men of the village stops to kibbitz, and as Charlie checks the carburetor the old man observes that it was not really much more work to catch enough fish to feed a dog team. He recalls for Jim and Charlie the years when he had one of the finest dog teams in the village. He had won races with those dogs, nine of them, all beauties. He reminisces about the time he was lost in a storm and the dogs could not find the trail. They had huddled together, burrowed into the snow, to keep warm. The storm went on and on, and he had grown very hungry. Finally, because there was no other way, he had killed one of the dogs and eaten him. Later another dog had died. But then the old man had been rescued. With a snow machine, that kind of survival is not possible, he says. If it breaks down on the trail, it will not keep you warm, and you can't eat it. Sled dogs would not break down. Jim listens politely until the old man limps away on frostbitten feet. He has heard the story before, many times.

Next Andy comes by, lugging a sack full of smelt, caught by fishing through holes cut in the ice, and announces that there will probably not be much more ice fishing this year. Soon the ice will be too thick to cut through, and the fish will be gone. Here near the Bering Sea coast the season lasts only through October and November when the fish—mostly tomcod and smelt and some ugly devil fish—are running upstream. In some places, ice fishing—also called hooking or jigging—lasts all through the winter, although toward spring the fish are lean and watery and tasteless.

Nearly everybody in the village goes hooking. In the fall when the ice first begins to form, the kids check the ice daily. When it's four inches thick, the word is out: "We can go hooking." Almost anything will do: a piece of string tied on a stick with a fishhook, or maybe a homemade hook like a bobbypin bent out and sharpened, and something red tied to the hook as a lure. Some people fish without any bait; others bring some, or use a mouthful of fish bitten out from under the gills. They dig a hole through the ice about the size of a basketball hoop, drop in the hook, and jiggle the line.

The children do it every chance they get, during recess, lunch hour—keeping the fish they catch in plastic bags or gunny sacks in the school entryway—or on the way home from school. The old women have endless patience for hooking. They squat or sit on stools by the holes in the ice with a tarp thrown over a tipped-over sled to protect themselves from the wind, a box of food, and a little camp stove for making tea. Through the hole in the ice, cleared of the new skin that formed since the last session, they dangle a stick decorated with feathers or certain plant stems. The tomcod is a stupid fish and will snap at anything that attracts its attention. When the fish go for the lure, the woman works a net with her free hand and scoops the fish out of the water—often four or five at a time go for a lure —and onto the ice, where they soon freeze. She catches hundreds of fish that way. Some of them will be stored in the fish house, some fried or boiled for supper.

When Andy reaches home, his first target is a fresh can of Copenhagen snuff. Like most of the children in the village, Andy has been using snuff since he was very small. Even his little sister Mary keeps a pinch under her lip, making a few discreet trips to the rest room at school to spit the brown juice into the sink. Most of the adults chew a mixture of tobacco and the ashes of low-growing willows that have been collected and burned.

Andy finds his mother drinking tea with some of her friends. They, too, have spent several hours out on the ice. Later Anna comes by alone. Now obviously pregnant, she's not allowed to go hooking; she's expected to stay home and take care of herself, and she's rather glad. It's bitterly cold on the ice. She left Christine at home with Carl, who is delighted that Anna is pregnant again, for he is positive that now he will get his son. Things have been going a little better with Anna and Carl. He has promised that he will not drink again, and although she knows that he will probably break the promise, she is pleased that he is making the effort. On her way into her mother's house, Anna stops to talk with Andy. One of the women calls to her and waves her to come in. She must not stand in the doorway like that, they tell her, or the baby will come only halfway out when she is in labor. Anna obeys; although she doesn't agree with some of the superstitious beliefs of the old women, she would not dispute them.

Even Father William has just about given up trying to argue them out of their superstitions. A few years ago during a severe storm, several young men were lost somewhere out on the tundra, and for two days search parties were unable to find them. The townspeople were grief-stricken. Nothing like that had happened in this village for a long time. The priest had tried to comfort them. We can only wait and pray, he told them. The rest is in God's hands; perhaps He is trying to teach us something.

But the old people of the church knew very well what had happened: God was punishing them for a specific sin. This young priest, in his enthusiasm for preserving the old ways of the culture, had asked some of the elderly men to sing their Eskimo songs at one of the masses. The men had done it, but now it was clear to the old women that they should not have: that was part of the old way, and it was not pleasing to God. They had learned this from the former priests a long time ago. God wanted them to forget about their old ways and to think only about Him and His Son. So He had caused the young men to become lost. The old men felt guilty, and Father William did his best to convince them that there was no connection. He could not persuade them; instead, they confessed their sin, and he absolved them. A day later the young men were found, and all survived.

On Sunday morning, Pete goes early to church. Father William has asked him to serve at the mass. Andy tags along, and the priest smiles when he sees him. "Next year, Andy, you will be serving." Andy grins broadly.

Andy is preparing for his First Communion. Every Thursday afternoon he attends catechism lessons at the parish house. The catechism is in English, and he does not always understand what it is about. He has learned to recite the Hail Mary and the Act of Contrition in English, since the priest listens to these, but the rest of the prayers he memorizes in Yupik.

The church is fuller than usual, because the students are home from Bethel, but the entire town always shows up for Sunday mass, which Father William celebrates in English. One of the women plays a small chord organ, and the congregation sings hymns that have been translated from English into Yupik. Not everyone present is there out of religious conviction, however; like many things done in Chaputnuak, a few people are there because of social pressure—they know that they would be gossiped about if they were absent.

Father William was sent to Chaputnuak five years ago from Hooper Bay, a much larger village farther north along the coast. He has grown to love the village and its people, although at times they mystify him and at other times they frustrate him. Father Gregory who served before him was old-fashioned in his ideas and paternalistic in his attitudes. He saw the Eskimos as children. It did not seem to occur to him that their culture had a value of its own; instead, he imposed his own ideas and tastes on them, and quite successfully. Father William confronted a wall of resistance when he tried to get his parishioners to replace the plastic Stations of the Cross with native artwork, and when he first suggested that the words on the altar linens might be embroidered in Yupik rather than in Latin. They were convinced that the garish examples of gussak religious art were the *right* way.

But Father William knows that his village has preserved far more of its ancient culture than has Shnamute, the Moravian village that is Chaputnuak's nearest neighbor. The Moravians are strongly opposed to gambling, drinking, card playing, and dancing—even traditional Eskimo dancing. Many young people come from Shnamute by snow machine to visit Chaputnuak, where the atmosphere is not so repressive. When the Shnamute teen-agers have the chance, they seem to go wild. Father William believes that parents in his parish have fewer problems with their children, because they are less restrictive.

Old Father Gregory warned the idealistic young priest not to be deceived by the apparent piety of his charges. A lot of people, he claimed, still believe in shamanism—the world of spirits—that the church has been trying to stamp out for over a century. Father William was curious about that. He was determined to find out if it were true that vestiges of shamanism linger on.

The young priest is the kind of man who makes friends easily. He began visiting around as soon as he arrived, and within a short time he knew everyone in the village. He liked them, and they seemed to like him, too, and to trust him. One day when he was having tea at the Koonuks' house, he decided to ask them what they knew about the old religion. Charlie had struck him as one of the most intelligent men of the village, and he felt they had a good relationship. Father William searched for a way to phrase the question diplomatically, but finally he just blurted it out: "Is shamanism still practiced in the village? Does anyone still believe in the spirits?"

Charlie was silent and helped himself to another chew of tobacco. Liz went to check the pot on the stove to make more tea. At last Charlie shook his head and said that was something from a long time ago, that he really didn't know anything about it. He really couldn't say. He didn't know anyone who might be able to answer the question either. Father William swirled the last of his tea in the cup, zipped up his Air Force parka, and left awkwardly. And he never did find anyone who would answer his question, however he phrased it, with more than a smile and an evasion.

Yet he has seen for himself that remnants of the old religion still persist. He is reminded of that every time a baby is brought to him for baptism. The baby is invariably named for a relative or a friend who has recently died. This is not merely the custom of honoring a beloved dead one, he realizes; they believe that the spirit of the one who has died must be passed on to a newborn. He does not argue with them; he simply explains that a baby must be given a Christian baptismal name as well as an Eskimo name, and everyone is satisfied.

Before the arrival of white men, Eskimos did not make a distinction between the natural world and the supernatural world of spirits. Because their survival depended not only on their skill as hunters but also on the availability of game that had more to do with luck than anything else, they observed a number of rituals and taboos to be sure there would be plenty of animals to kill. They believed that animals, like people, had spirits; if the animal spirits were displeased, they would not allow themselves to be hunted.

The Eskimos also believed in reincarnation among animals; the spirit of the dead animal floated off to inhabit the body of a newly born animal. If that spirit were not pleased with the hunter and his people, the animal in which it had taken up residence would not allow itself to be killed. One way to please the spirit was to treat the dead or dying animal with respect; a seal was offered a drink of water just before or after it died, and the throat of the animal was cut to release its soul. These traditions may still be practiced in some villages, but the people of Chaputnuak now dismiss them as impractical.

Sometimes when game animals were scarce, the people believed that hunters or someone in the village had broken one of the rules and that the spirits were angry.

They would try to make amends to the offended spirits, usually under the direction of a shaman. Before the coming of Christianity, the shaman was a powerful person in the village. The equivalent of the African witch doctor or the Indian medicine man, he claimed to have mystical contact with the world of invisible spirits, and he acted as an intermediary between the people of his village and the supernatural spirit world. His people believed he had the power to protect them from these mysterious spirits.

The shaman—a name that originated among Siberian tribes and means "he who knows"—was usually a highly intelligent person with characteristics that set him apart: he was a loner in a society where people tended to live closely, a sensitive and highly emotional person who showed tears and anger in a society that values emotional control. Some shamans had unusual physical characteristics, such as a stutter. Not all shamans were forces for good, however; there are stories of shamans who became dangerous and met violent ends. But whether good or evil, they were extremely influential people.

It was to this religion that the first Christian missionaries turned their attention. In one way or another they tried to eliminate shamanism and to substitute Christianity in its place. What often happened, though, was that Christianity became a kind of addition, rather than a total substitution. God the Father, Son, and Holy Ghost were additional spirits that had to be pleased. Some of the elderly people believed that the old spirits were angered when people turned their attention to Christ. The new Christians, still frightened by what they had turned away from, became pious Christians in order to please Jesus, hoping He would protect them from evil that could be done to them by the rejected spirits who were still not completely forgotten.

Andy is getting ready for his First Communion. He goes to church often, studies his catechism willingly, and looks forward to the big day. His mother is making him new mukluks for the occasion, and his father has promised that he will have a new suit, complete with a shirt and necktie. It will be the biggest thing in his life since he killed his first bird and will be celebrated in much the same way. The parents of the children in the catechism class will get together and give a dinner in the community center, in honor of Andy and his friends.

For the first time in his school years in Bethel, Jim is looking forward to going back after Thanksgiving. The reason is a girl, Ilena Wassily, from the village of Russian Mission. Ilena is not like any girl he has ever known, and Jim marvels at her ideas and ambitious plans. She says that she intends to go to college. She will stay in Bethel and attend the Kuskokwim Community College for two years, and then she will go to the University of Alaska to get her teaching degree. After that she will return to her village and teach in the school. By the time she is ready to teach, she says, the BIA will be on the way out. The villages have taken over their own schools. And who should be teaching in those schools anyway? Not gussaks. The white people in Bethel are very nice and very helpful, and Ilena feels that she has learned a lot from them. But she is determined to be a teacher in her own village school, where she will teach the children what they need to know about being Eskimos, and not about being potato farmers in Maine.

Jim does not like being told such things by a girl. These are things that an older man might say to him, his eyes hidden in the darkness of the steam bath, not a young girl with shining black hair and a T-shirt with the name of a singing group stenciled on the front. But she is kind and her smile is gentle. Jim feels his mother would like her.

Ilena has told him about the Russian Orthodox Church to which her family belongs. Even their calendar is different, she says: they use the Julian calendar, and their holidays are not celebrated on the same dates as the Catholics and Protestants. Christmas is on January 7, and Easter, too, always comes later.

Ilena is interested in Eskimo crafts. She knows how to make baskets and do beadwork, and now she is learning how to carve dolls and sew skin outfits for them. She says it is important for Eskimos to practice skills from their past, and she is trying to get Jim involved in the cultural heritage program, special classes at school about old ways and how to preserve them. The class publishes a yearly book called *Kaliikaq Yugnek* (Book About People), and Ilena is on the staff. She has been interviewing some of the old women in her village and in Bethel to learn from them about some of the old traditions and stories. One of her classmates does drawings for the book, and they would like Jim to work on the project too. The day before he left for Thanksgiving vacation, Ilena asked him to find out everything he could about trapping and promised to help him write an article about it. "You can have your name on the article," she said.

One day the curator of the Bethel museum, *Yugtarvik* (meaning "The Place of the People's Things"), brought to the school a skin kayak that was part of an exhibit at the museum. The dry heat of the building had dried out the boat, causing the skin to shrink until the wood frame began to break. The curator had bought six new seal skins, rounded up some workers, and set up the restoration project in the high school lounge where everyone could watch. Ilena and Jim spent all their free time in the lounge while the men repaired the wooden frame, lashing each rib to a crosspiece. Six women sewed the damp sealskins together with sinew, working quickly before the skins dried out again and became too difficult to sew. Then the men pulled the skin covering over the wooden frame and sewed it in place. This time, to keep the skins from shrinking, they rubbed it carefully inside and out with warm oil, as they did when kayaks were used by all seal hunters.

One of the men explained to the attentive students what it used to be like to hunt in a kayak. The hunter sat inside the opening, which was shaped like a barrel hoop. Then he put on a raincoat made of seal intestine and tied it tightly around the hoop and around his face. That way he formed one unit with the boat, so that if it tipped over no water could go in, and he stayed dry. He practiced rolling over and over in the kayak, tipping over to one side and coming up on the other. If he had mastered this "roll," he would not drown.

The kayak is good, the Eskimo told the students. These light, maneuverable skin boats can go many places that wooden boats can't, and you can carry them, if you have to. There's plenty of space inside, room for several small seals, and if the water gets rough and you happen to tip over, you won't lose the seals. In many villages kayaks are still in use.

Listening and watching, Jim remembered last spring when he went seal hunting with his uncles and how embarrassed he was because they seemed so old-fashioned to him. Now his embarrassment is being replaced slowly with pride in the old ways. He has always liked seal hunting and fishing and trapping, but now he is beginning to see that being Eskimo goes beyond that. Language, music, crafts —all of it counts.

When the plane lands in Bethel a few days after Thanksgiving, Jim can hardly wait to see Ilena again—to tell her all about building mink traps, of course.

December

"HO HO HO!"

A man in a fake white beard and a shabby red suit stuffed with pillows stands uneasily on a makeshift platform at one end of the schoolroom. It would be hard to find a place in the United States where a folk figure with a workshop at the North Pole and a sled drawn by reindeer should be more appropriate, but this Santa Claus looks definitely uncomfortable.

Santa has a big job ahead of him tonight, distributing the mountain of gifts stacked around the schoolroom. Nearly every family in the village exchanges presents at Christmas, and all of them have been brought here, two days before Christmas, for the big event of the holiday season.

Tonight is the climax of days of preparation. In the

past, the women had spent most of the darkening days of fall making new mukluks for everybody in the family, and usually new parkas, too. The urge to have everything new for the season is still strong, but in recent years the people of villages like Chaputnuak have come to rely more on the mail-order catalogues than on their skills with the needle. The new parkas the children will receive this year are more likely to be down-filled than fur. Like many of the girls, Louise has asked for a pair of sleek leather boots, rather than mukluks. Still, sewing machines have been humming steadily and knitting needles clicking for the past month. Louise has produced a pair of patterned mittens for each member of her family.

Louise has spent today fixing her hair, which now lies in puffs on her shoulders. She is wearing a white sweater saved for special occasions and has applied her make-up with great care—all of this to come to the Christmas program with her family, to watch Mary and Andy say their pieces. All through the exercises her brother Evon wriggles and bounces on her lap. She whispers to him to keep still, but it doesn't work, and he crows with pleasure when Mary takes her place in front of the audience. She and the other second graders huddle together in a knot, the girls giggling nervously. Mary has practiced and practiced her piece, but when the time comes to recite the poem she is so nervous she covers her face with her hands. Her parents smile at her encouragingly, and finally she whispers the words.

When Andy's turn comes with his group, he stands very straight and stares over the heads of the audience. Em-

Snow machines
have replaced dog teams
in most of southwestern Alaska,
except for special
racing events.

barrassment made Mary giggle and blush, but it turns Andy to stone. He repeats his piece clearly, without error —and without expression in his voice or on his face.

The program moves along slowly. Each child has something to say, each group has a carol to sing. During one of the carols, Charlie Koonuk slips out of the room and struggles into the Santa Claus costume. Everybody knows that Charlie has been doing the Santa act for as long as he has been maintenance man for the school. It seems to be part of the job; being on the village council is double reinforcement. A few men come forward to act as Santa's helpers, and within a half-hour each family has accumulated an impressive mound of packages. With a final burst of "Ho-ho-ho's," Santa departs and Charlie Koonuk reappears. Soon the schoolroom is filled with a welter of wrapping paper, ribbons, and boxes, and a chorus of appreciative murmurs.

Louise gets a new blue pants outfit and the boots she wanted so much; she intends to wear them when she goes to Shnamute with the family next week for a visit. Andy is thrilled to get a pair of skis. There is not much place for skiing on the flat tundra, but the children like to drag their sleds to the top of the snow drifts around the houses. Sometime this winter Mr. McGrath will take the boys by snow machine to the low hill that bulges up from the tundra a few miles from town and let them slide down on pieces of plastic. Andy means to take his skis along, after he's had time to practice on the drifts.

Pete has been given a fine new gun. He manages

somehow to suppress his excitement, but he is already picturing how he is going to get his first seal with this gun. Jim finds a camera and some film and flashbulbs have been wrapped for him. "So you can work on that book for the high school," his father says.

Mary unwraps a doll made of plastic with curly brown hair and blue eyes that open and close. Store-bought dolls are not common in the village. Her mother has sewed a little *qaspeq* for it and made tiny fur mukluks. It all looks a bit odd on the gussak doll, but Mary is delighted with her baby, and she cuddles it happily. The littlest ones, Evon and Christine, get new outfits. Anna receives presents for the baby due in March—boxes of disposable diapers, blankets, and so on. And Liz and Charlie give her and Carl a set of delicate blue-flowered china dishes, four of everything.

And then there are presents from all the relatives. This year seems to be the year for religious pictures, and each family has given and received at least one large colored portrait of Christ at Gethsemane or Christ Knocking at the Door. Grandmothers have knitted caps for the children, men have bought ammunition and tools for brothers and cousins, women have wrapped sheets and towels and kitchen equipment for each other. In addition to all the family exchanges, the teachers present each child with a small, inexpensive book. For many children, this is the first and only book they have, except for comic books. Andy's is about birds of North America: robins, blue jays, orioles. He cannot find any ptarmigan.

Care has been taken not to omit anyone and not to give gifts that might earn the giver a reputation for stinginess. As a result, a huge amount of cash has flowed out of this small village to the big mail-order companies, and each household now has more objects to tax its limited storage space. But it has been a big, joyous occasion, and everyone seems pleased with the gifts. After the McGraths serve the usual fruit punch and cookies, the program is over. Each family loads its horde of new possessions into the sled behind the snow machine and heads for home. Evon, clutching a small rubber toy, sleeps on Louise's shoulder.

Christmas Eve: only two days past the winter solstice, the dark sky turns gray late in the morning, brightens around noon, then fades to darkness by midafternoon. It is the village custom on this, one of the longest nights of the year, to run the generators all night, and every house glows with light.

At midnight the entire village turns out for midnight mass. Father William appears in his festive regalia. His surplice looks strikingly like ermine, but he enjoys explaining its humbler origins: black dots applied with a felt-tip pen to white rabbit fur. Candles blaze in whalebone holders around the church, and one of the high school boys plays his guitar during the offertory.

When the mass is over, the young people drift next door to the community center for their all-night dance. The rest of the villagers, older and younger, visit at each other's homes, enjoying the luxury of all-night electricity. It seems characteristic of Eskimos that they can adjust their pattern of sleep with little effort. During the summer when the light lasts through the night, they stay up very late. In the spring, when seal hunting season is at its peak, they are out for long periods at a time, snatching only a few hours of sleep before they go out again. But mostly during the long nights of winter, they sleep—except on special occasions like Christmas. Then they stay together for hours, telling stories of past Christmases, reviving old memories.

The day after Christmas when Louise hears the roar of the mail plane, she throws on her parka and rushes off to see what might have come in. The home of Moses Kiyutelluk is one of the most frequently visited in the village. Moses is the official postmaster of Chaputnuak, a far more demanding job in the village of two hundred souls than one might suppose.

Officially Chaputnuak has three-times-a-week mail service from Bethel, a schedule that is disrupted more often than not by weather conditions. Sometimes mail piles up on both ends of the run for several weeks at a time when winter storms rage or while spring breakup turns the airstrip to an unmanageable slush too muddy for ordinary wheels, the river too full of ice for floats, the snow too soft for skis. Christmas cards and presents from relatives in other villages are often weeks late in arriving, although older villagers remember when the only mail the village got was delivered by the summer barge.

Kiyutelluk had been the postmaster for years, and there were some complaints that he really wasn't doing a good job. He was supposed to be present for certain hours each day at the post office, a space in the community center equipped with a counter, scales, cashbox, and a series of wooden pigeonholes into which Moses sorted the mail. But since he was rarely there during the posted hours, people began to stop by at his home to ask for their mail or to get some help in addressing an outgoing package. When the customers came, Kiyutelluk's wife Martha would put on her parka and mukluks, rummage for the keys, and then slowly, her joints showing reluctance, make her way to the post office, since Kiyutelluk himself was very often "away" —supposedly hunting, fishing, or trapping, but actually sleeping.

One day a crudely lettered sign appeared on the door of the community center: P.O. MOVED TO MARTHAS HOUSE. Outside the door of the Kiyutelluk dwelling another sign listed the post office hours. Inside, Martha sat smiling at her kitchen table behind an array of scales and rubber stamps. From then on, Martha was self-appointed acting postmaster, and all post office business was conducted in her kitchen.

It is usually Louise who goes for the mail. With long hours to while away without much to do except look after Evon and sometimes her niece Christine, Louise has developed a time-consuming correspondence with friends and cousins in other villages. Every week she sends out a half-dozen letters and gets about as many in return. But today Martha hands her a bundle of fifteen envelopes, nearly all of them addressed to her. Her family is intending to go to Shnamute during Christmas vacation, and many plans are in the making.

A few days later when the weather promises to stay clear, Charlie finishes tinkering with his snow machine, gasses up, and hooks the homemade wooden sled to the back of it for Liz and Mary and Evon. Jim borrows his uncle's snow machine and sled, in which Louise bounces along with Andy and Pete. It's a cold, rough ride, even though they have dressed in their warmest parkas, and there is a tarp to pull over Liz and the younger children to protect them from the wind. A few other families are going, too, and soon a caravan is strung out over the tundra, following tripods of sticks that mark the trail to the next village.

The trail is in good condition, and in a little over an hour Jim has picked out the cluster of dots that is Shnamute. With nearly twice the population of Chaputnuak, Shnamute somehow seems more prosperous, too. The paint on the houses looks brighter, the colors of the wash on the clotheslines seem gayer, the snow machines are bigger and newer. The caravan sweeps into the village over the frozen pond and scatters among the homes of relatives, who greet them warmly and put the teakettle on to boil. Louise takes Mary and goes to find her letter-writing friends, to show them the new clothes she got for Christmas and to admire theirs. Liz and Evon visit with the women, Charlie with the men, Jim and Pete and Andy with the boys. Later Charlie teases Liz about her "gossiping."

"And what do *you* do?" Liz wants to know.

"That's different," Charlie explains. "Women gossip; men tell stories."

That night they eat in whatever house they happen

to be stopping and sleep wherever there is space. But the next morning Charlie is anxious to get started for home; the weather is changing, and it could be dangerous out there. Louise and her friends promise to see each other again in a few weeks—first at a potlatch in Chaputnuak, later at the Moravian church rally in Shnamute. The caravan manages to arrive home in time to avoid a major winter storm.

Christine is one year old on December 30, and to celebrate the birthday of his first child, Carl decides to have a men's party. Although birthdays are not generally observed, a fuss is sometimes made for the firstborn child.

Carl invites most of the young men and some of the older men, including his father-in-law, to his home for a dinner. All day long Anna does the best she can to clean and straighten up their little house, sweeping, carting out trash, trying to make it look better than it is. Anna is not much of a housekeeper and her house is a poor one to begin with, so she has much to do simply to make it neat. There is nothing she can do, she finally admits to herself, to make it look attractive as well.

Liz comes to help her with the cooking; she and Anna will be the only women present. Around suppertime the men begin to arrive. Carl, the proud father and jovial host, enjoys serving them a huge meal of boiled mink from his father-in-law's fish house. The few pieces of shabby furniture have been pushed out of the way, and the men sit on the floor, eating and talking. After the meal they take turns washing their hands and faces in the basin of water that Anna set by the oven to warm. Meanwhile Anna and Liz brew the tea and serve the pilot bread and *akutaq* that Liz has prepared. After the tea, Carl divides up the leftover food, giving a share to each, starting with the older men. Then he brings out tobacco, penknives, and other small items as gifts for his guests. There is such a lot to give away —too much, Anna feels, considering that they have so little money. After the gifts have been handed out, the men congratulate him once more on his fine daughter, tease him about the destined arrival of a son, and go home.

But not everybody leaves. Among the guests is Carl's brother Steve who came down from a village to the north with a load of gifts—all of it in bottles. Carl and Steve began drinking when the men's party ends. They drink through the night until early morning, when they finally pass out.

Carl's drinking pattern is typical of the Eskimo culture in general, in the remote villages as well as in the large cities, a pattern so common and destructive that alcoholism is probably the leading health problem among them. In the past twenty-five years the rate of deaths from alcohol has multiplied by five among Alaskan natives. Carl is a binge drinker, rather than a steady drinker, partly because alcohol is not regularly available. There is no such thing as "social drinking"—having a cocktail or two before a meal or during the evening. When he does get hold of a bottle—vodka is his favorite, whisky is acceptable, and anything at all will do once he gets started—Carl drinks his liquor straight, either until the bottle is empty, or until he passes out. Once he begins to drink, there is no stopping him.

Anna cries silently in her bed. Carl had promised that he would not drink any more, but she knew when she saw Steve and the bottles of vodka that he would not be able to refuse the gift or resist the insistence that he drink. It became then a question of manhood, and there was no doubt what would happen. He could not tell his brother that he had decided not to drink. Steve would know it was because of Anna, that she had persuaded him to make the promise. He would tease Carl, calling him an old woman, saying his wife was the boss.

The cap comes off another bottle at noon the next day when a few friends stop by and roust the brothers out of their stupefied sleep. For the first few drinks they are jovial, full of cheer for an early-starting New Year's Eve. They urge Anna to join them, but she refuses. When Carl calls her ugly names, she picks up the baby and runs to her father's house. She does not want to tell her parents what's wrong, and when suppertime comes she eats with them, using little Christine to distract them from her own problems. She sees her father looking at her once, but no questions are asked. She and the baby spend the evening there.

When the Koonuks go to midnight mass, it is evident from the poor turnout that many other families are dealing with similar problems. After the service Anna's father offers to walk home with her, but she shakes her head. The little house is cold when she gets there. She turns up the stove and waits. Soon Carl staggers in, kisses her drunkenly, and tries again to get her to drink with him. Again she refuses. When she begins to cry and Christine starts to whimper, Carl digs into the cardboard box where the new dishes her parents gave them for Christmas are still packed. One by one, he smashes them against the wall, yelling that he will quit when she promises to be a good wife and do as he says. When Anna tries to stop him, he slaps her and sends her sprawling.

After Carl slams out of the house, Anna slowly begins to clean up the mess, sweeping the broken china into a big pile in the middle of the floor. Only one piece is unbroken —a cup, and Anna makes herself tea to drink from it. Outside her window she can see her husband racing with his friends on their snow machines. New Year's celebrants are running in and out of some of the houses, and there is raucous laughter and shouting all over the village. Through the long night Anna sits at the window, listening and watching. Later, when the race is over, she sees Carl tear by once more, this time with a woman behind him on the seat. Anna recognizes her: Daisy White, a widow in her forties who has had two children since her husband froze to death outside a bar in Bethel a half-dozen years ago. Daisy too is a heavy drinker, and the men in town all know she will accept their sexual advances when she has been drinking. Carl and Daisy careen through the village to her house. His snow machine is still parked there a few hours later when Anna takes Christine to visit her parents.

Alcoholism is a serious problem in Chaputnuak, as it is in nearly every Eskimo village, and the council has passed a number of laws in an attempt to control drinking. No liquor is sold in the village, but until Bethel was voted dry a few years ago, it was a simple matter to have a bottle or a case sent out by plane. After that source was shut off, people began to order from shops in Anchorage. Now there is talk of outlawing liquor by mail. This will certainly make drinking more expensive; the Bethel bootleggers charge very high prices.

There are other laws, too: appearing drunk in public in Chapunuak means arrest and a fine—twenty dollars for the first offense, fifty for the second, a hundred for the third, and fourth offenders are asked to leave town. But it is known that the laws are invoked with discretion; some of the men have paid "third-offense" fines a half-dozen times or more. Anna is not sure what "in public" means. Carl often gets drunk with his friends at the pool hall and staggers home raging at her. Although he has been warned several times, Carl has never been arrested—probably because he is Charlie Koonuk's son-in-law.

Nearly every family in town has at least one member with a drinking problem. There are known drinkers on the town council that makes the laws, and the enforcement officer is also a drinker. Furthermore, the villagers are reluctant to press charges. It's a tiny place; the embarrassment of wrongdoing should be enough.

One of the worst results of alcoholism is child abuse. All too often both parents become involved in drinking, and then the children are neglected, often left alone for days while the parents are on a binge. Sometimes the husbands and wives attack each other physically, and sometimes the children are beaten, too.

Before the arrival of the white man, Eskimos had no intoxicating liquors, and they did not have the stress of living within two cultures. Although Eskimos seem to have a physical intolerance for alcohol, the psychological attraction to it is strong. The traditional Eskimo was a person who had learned to live in balance with the most hostile environment in the world. But the modern Eskimo sees himself mainly in relation to the *white man's* culture, and his self-image is bound to be negative. Drinking helps him forget his feelings of worthlessness and of his increasing dependence on someone else's culture. An Eskimo is taught from early childhood to control his feelings, to suppress his anger and cover up his hostility. But when he drinks, his inhibitions disappear, and the pent-up anger erupts with a roar. Furthermore, drinking lets him deny responsibility for his actions: "I didn't know what I was doing."

The pattern begins early, often in high school. In the cities it may end up in prostitution and pimping. In the villages it's a cycle of drinking, fighting, sobering up, apologizing or shrugging it off, and waiting for the next opportunity. Self-respect dwindles, and the binges come oftener. Nothing seems to matter any more. The spiral winds steadily downward and often ends in suicide. The rate of suicide among natives has doubled since 1950.

By noon on New Year's Day most of the excitement has died down. Whatever liquor was brought into the village has been consumed, and the drinkers are sleeping off their hangovers. Family fights have subsided, and even for those who have fought most bitterly, everything is forgiven if not yet forgotten. It is not in the Eskimo character to hold a grudge, and nearly everyone deliberately puts out of mind any unpleasantness that might mar the beginning of the new year. The families take their food to the community center to share the feast, and as always the children are the focus of attention. Carl, his body heavy with fatigue and his eyes aching, holds his little daughter tenderly on his lap and feeds her tiny bits of food from his plate.

Anna watches her husband and her daughter, and she feels the stirrings of another life within her. Maybe this will be a better year for them. Maybe Carl will make a new promise. Maybe this time he'll keep it.

January

ALTHOUGH THE FLAME ROARS IN THE OIL STOVE AND THE
stack-robber blows hot air from the stovepipe in the direction of Liz's elegant sofa, the Koonuks' house is drafty and
chilly. Through December the temperature averaged fifteen degrees below zero, but now it is dropping and the
windchill factor drags it down to a brutal fifty below. The
plane to take the high school students back to Bethel after
Christmas vacation has been delayed by the high winds.

Pleased to have Jim and Pete with them for at least
one more day, the family has drawn around the stove to eat
supper. When they are finishing, their Uncle David ducks
under the blanket that keeps snow from blowing from the
porch into the house and slams the porch door hard behind
him against the cold. He walked only a few yards from his
own house, but his parka is covered with snow crystals.

Although he says he has just eaten supper, tea is poured for him and a dish of *akutaq* set out. Soon he begins to tell one of his stories, and without a word, Liz switches off the bright overhead light to set the mood.

Jim and Pete thoroughly enjoy their uncle's visits and his storytelling, even though they have heard it all many times before. David speaks softly, his voice rising and falling as he creates the scene and the action. His audience attentively follows his gestures, the inflection of his voice, the changes of facial expression, the dramatic pauses. The semi-darkness, the cold outside, and the interest of the people gathered around him combine to heighten the excitement and tension. The whole family is under the storyteller's spell.

Storytelling is important in Eskimo culture for several reasons. Probably the main one is its entertainment value: it's a good way to pass a long winter night. But it is also a way to pass along Eskimo history and legends. Some of these stories attempt to explain the big questions of how the universe works and the relationship of people with their environment. Some deal with cultural ideas of right and wrong.

Uncle David has a tale that he saves for times when Jim and Pete are around, because he enjoys the expression on their faces when he tells it. The story is about an old woman who lived alone and was always hungry because there was no one to hunt for her, and the people in the village never brought her food. In the same village lived two brothers, successful young hunters, and the old woman

Village men beat
traditional rhythms
on gut-covered driftwood.

decided to marry one of them. She washed her face, fixed her hair as best she could, and went to the boys' home with her proposal: if one of them would marry her, she would cook for him. When one of the boys asked his father's permission, the older man refused, asking his son why he wanted to marry a woman old enough to be his mother. The answer made the old woman angry. Later, when the villagers moved to another place, the old woman put up her tent far away from the others. She made a statue of a bear and sent the bear's spirit to kill the father. Just before he died, the father told his sons to take his body to the old woman's tent, along with a bow and arrow. The next day the old woman was found dead with an arrow in her heart.

When David finishes that story, Charlie thinks of one to tell, this about a man who found a creature that was half-worm and half-woman with a beauty dot between her eyes. He took her home with him, and as he cared for her she gradually became less and less an ugly worm and more and more an attractive woman. But one day while he was out hunting, another man came and shot her with an arrow through the beauty dot. Heartbroken, her protector moved away to another place.

Later, after Uncle David leaves and the family gets ready to sleep, Pete lies in his sleeping bag and thinks of the stories. He knows that long ago, when people often had several husbands and wives in a lifetime, men often married women much older than they who were experienced in preparing meat and making skin clothing. Still, he could not imagine it; it was easier to imagine a worm turning into a woman.

A woman performs
graceful movements
with her dance fans.

Uncle David is known in the village for the stories he makes up, yet he like other storytellers draws most often from a fund of traditional tales that have their roots somewhere deep in the past of the Eskimo people, a past that reaches back from four to six thousand years to the arrival of their first ancestors on this continent.

Many thousands of years ago, a bridge of land connected the continents of North America and Asia and separated the Bering Sea from the Arctic Ocean. This land bridge, named Beringia by geologists, has submerged and emerged at various times in the earth's history as the level of the Bering Sea has risen and fallen. As a result, a rich accumulation of the remains of sea animals and plants produced a lush vegetation that lured animals such as the caribou across the bridge from the pastures of Siberia to the continent of North America, and the nomadic people of East Asia who followed the game came after them.

Anthropologists believe that both Eskimos and American Indians trace their ancestry to East Asia, but because there is little similarity between the two groups, scientists have concluded that they migrated at different times. The Indians, who probably crossed the land bridge about twenty-five thousand years ago, spread east across Canada and south throughout what is now the United States.

Thousands of years passed, and water covered the land bridge again. Then some four to six thousand years ago, another group of East Asians migrated to North America, either by paddling boats from Siberia across the fifty-six-mile strait of open water or by walking over the ice that sometimes jammed the strait. These more recent immigrants had physical characteristics markedly different from the earlier group. Their light skin, short, broad noses, and almond-shaped eyes narrowed by the mongoloid fold that covers the inner corner of the eye are all Oriental characteristics that developed in Asia *after* the earlier migration of people from whom the American Indian descended. Most Eskimos could easily be mistaken for Japanese.

While the early arrivals were probably following game, such as the caribou, the reasons for the later group making the arduous trip are not clear. For whatever reason, the ancestors of the people who made their home in the farthest north and whom we call Eskimos (from an Indian word meaning "raw fish eaters") arrived on the coast of western Alaska some time before 2000 B.C., the time from which the oldest known Eskimo artifacts can be dated. One group separated from the rest and spread throughout the Aleutian Islands, where they eventually evolved their own language and culture, distinct from but related to the Eskimos.

Most of the people traveled eastward across Canada and into Greenland. There were several waves of migration; among the earliest was a group known as the Dorsets who reached northern Newfoundland. Later came the Thule culture (pronounced THOO-lee) along the Arctic Coast who used skin boats—one-man kayaks and larger *umiaks*—to hunt aquatic mammals. The Thules were an advanced and prosperous culture who invented the dog-sled. This gave them a greater mobility than they had ever had, and by about A.D. 1000 they and their Eskimo descendants inhabited the entire coast of the American Arctic. Always during these ancient times there were bloody clashes with the North American Indians, who were vastly superior warriors. Eventually peace was restored when the Eskimos adapted to life along the coast, leaving the wooded interior to the Indians. Even today the relationship between Indians and Eskimos is an uneasy one.

Today there are close to eighty thousand Eskimos in the world, and the population is on the increase. Nearly half of them are in Greenland, and a reverse migration to the Chukchi Peninsula in Siberia established a small population there. When Peter Freuchen, the Danish explorer, wrote his famous *Book of the Eskimos* in the 1950s, he set the number of Eskimos in Alaska at 16,000; by the 1960s it had risen to 22,000; according to the U.S. census of 1970, there were 28,233 Eskimos in Alaska. The native population of Alaska, including Eskimos, Aleuts, and Indians, is growing almost twice as fast as that of the U.S. as a whole at the rate of two percent annually. This increase at a rate comparable to East Asia's may be due to the custom of large families and greatly reduced infant mortality. Three-quarters of the Alaskan Eskimos are under thirty-five.

About eight centuries before the arrival of the Russian explorers in Alaska, the Eskimos of Greenland and Newfoundland were the first of the native North Americans to be contacted by western Europeans: Norsemen who referred to this first American minority group with the derisive term of *skraelings*. During the precontact era when the Eskimo culture had reached its full development but had not yet come under the influence of Western civilization, Eskimo families moved their homes several times a year, following the seasonal availability of fish, sea mammals, and caribou. The Yupiks on the Bering Sea coast took their kayaks out into the sea to hunt for seal and whale and followed the broad Kuskokwim River and its tributaries, establishing temporary fish camps and then moving on when the food supply moved. One of these fish camps was called Mutrekhlagamiut, meaning "smokehouse people," referring to the peculiar way the villagers had of smoking their fish. In 1884 the Moravian missionaries arrived and gave the village the more (for them) pronounceable but less appropriate name of Bethel, meaning "house of God."

The northern Eskimos along the Arctic Coast called themselves *Inupiat,* which means the same as *Yupik:* The Real People. It was inevitable, given the area over which Eskimos are spread, that cultural as well as linguistic differences developed. What's surprising is that they have remained so similar.

The arrival of missionaries and traders began to change the living patterns of the Eskimos. Although they still followed their food supply, the desire for an education for their children and as a result of it a better, easier life for them, has conflicted strongly with their nomadic nature. Only a few of the Eskimo groups still move about as freely as they once did. The snow machine and the airplane have made it much easier to live in one place and to hunt and fish over a wide area.

It is a feeling for this past, rather than any specific knowledge of it, that shapes the storyteller's words.

The day after Uncle David's storytelling, there is a break in the weather. Mail arrives, and the students leave for Bethel with the usual tearful farewells. The next official vacation is not until Easter, although some of the boys may make trips home before then, particularly if seal season begins.

The worst of the Arctic winter presses down on the tundra with long hours of darkness and days of extreme cold. For the next couple of months most of life will be lived indoors. Several afternoons a week, while the children are at school, both men and women gather at the community center to play bingo, the most popular form of daytime entertainment. One of the women calls the numbers, and the others sit on the floor and concentrate on their cards, sometimes as many as two dozen apiece. A lot of money changes hands during each session. Liz sometimes wins and sometimes loses; like most of the players, she believes that it comes out about even. Furthermore, it's fun.

Once in a while Liz and her friends get together in someone's home to play "snertz," a kind of multiple solitaire. Card-playing is nearly as well-liked as bingo, although poker (Eskimos have their own three-card version) and other forms of gambling are against the rules established by the town council. It's a rule that is often ignored, although it was made primarily for the young men who were sometimes gambling away their whole paychecks at the pool hall, leaving nothing with which to buy necessities for the family.

Conversation at the community center between bingo games is about Amelia's suggestion. Amelia, Liz's mother, has been telling them about a time years ago when the people of the village used to exchange names every winter. The women drew men's names and the men drew women's names; each gave a gift to the person whose name he drew. The women all say that it sounds like a fine idea, and before the bingo session has ended they agree, in typical Eskimo fashion, to think about it some more.

Then Daisy White, the middle-aged widow, suggests that maybe it's too much gift-giving, with the big potlatch coming up soon. The women do not have much respect for Daisy, and they would tend to disagree with her, very gently, on just about anything. This has nothing to do with the potlatch, they tell her. This is an individual thing, not like the massive exchange of gifts that will take place there. Daisy does not argue.

Within a week the matter of the gift exchange has been settled and the names are drawn. Nobody keeps the names a secret. Soon Charlie reports to Liz that Billy Green, the man in charge of the village generator, stopped him to ask what Liz would like. She is hard pressed to think of anything, but finally she mentions that she really needs a new jigger for ice fishing. And the next time Louise goes by the Kiyutelluks' house to pick up the mail, Martha mentions that Moses has always been a great admirer of her mother's knitting. Since Liz has Moses's name, perhaps a pair of gloves, with a design of a ptarmigan knitted into it? Charlie is in for some gentle teasing: he has drawn Daisy White's name, and Daisy has let him know she wants a fancy scarf from Egoak's store.

Meanwhile, everybody is getting ready for the potlatch, the high point of the winter, the biggest social event of the year. Calls have been coming in on the CB radios indicating that quite a few guests are coming from Shnamute to enjoy the traditional Eskimo dancing that is prohibited in their strict Moravian village. Guests are also expected from some of the villages to the north, although the distance is much greater and few will want to make the arduous trip of four or five hours by snow machine or pay the cost of flying down.

There is the usual concern about the weather, which has been typically stormy with relentless, howling winds, but on the last Friday in January the howl suddenly drops to a whisper. By midmorning the sky is quite bright, and by eleven o'clock a caravan of a dozen snow machines with sleds has swept into the village and dispersed among the houses. Suddenly, a couple of hours later, a ground blizzard kicks up, and swirling snow cuts visibility to zero. Anyone caught even a few feet from his house can lose his sense of direction and wander for hours, perhaps dying of exposure before he can find his way back.

Everyone is thinking of travelers who may be somewhere out on the trail. A call to villages to the north verifies the fact that a caravan did start out on the eighty-mile trip in the morning, but most had turned back when the weather changed. One group had kept on going.

When the ground blizzard stops as suddenly as it began, Carl and a few of his friends decide to go looking for them: the missing ones are from his home village. Late in the afternoon the people of Chaputnuak, watching from their houses, spot a swarm of bright headlamps approaching from the north. Soon the cold travelers are laughing over cups of hot tea. A snow machine had broken down— the fan belt had snapped, and although it is customary to carry an extra, the owner had forgotten to replace the spare after the last breakdown. While they tried to make do with an extra belt from one of the other machines in the group, the storm had struck. They had turned the sleds on their sides and pulled tarps over them to form a shelter, and there they had waited. The rescuers found them half-buried in drifting snow, but they were unharmed. The inflexible rule is that if something happens, stay put. Sometimes younger, less experienced men and teen-age boys forget the rule or deliberately ignore it and start to walk. Then, if a blizzard swirls in, they quickly lose the trail and with it all hope of rescue. They all remembered the boy from one of the villages who, three years ago at potlatch time, had broken the rule. He died in the storm, only a mile from the village.

But they are safe now, and they shrug off the danger. Carl and one of the men he helped rescue—a cousin—drift off toward the poolhall with a bottle of vodka. Time for a little celebration.

Late in the afternoon everyone in the village begins to get ready for the potlatch. Liz puts on her best parka, made of fox fur trimmed with bands of inlaid calfskin and decorated around the sleeves and hem with beadwork and mink tassels. She has had it for years, and she preserves it to wear for special occasions like this one. Mary has a new rabbit fur parka trimmed with fur from the muskrats Andy and her grandfather shot last June; her grandmother Frances gave it to her for Christmas. Louise also has a decorated parka, but she prefers to wear her new gussak clothes.

Meanwhile Charlie takes some smoked salmon and frozen whitefish from the fish house to the community center for the potlatch dinner and then goes back for a carton of canned fruits, crackers, tea bags, and sugar. Tonight the women are dancing, and by custom the men will prepare the food. During the dinner everybody is given a new nickname for the occasion, accompanied by much joking and teasing, a lot of it having to do with sex. Then the men clear away the remains of the food, and everyone finds a place to sit on the floor.

The dance begins. About a dozen women carrying dance fans made of feathers and fur and dressed in their finest furs congregate in a room just outside the main hall. Five men sit with their flat drums, a gut covering stretched taut over a circular driftwood rim. They begin to drum softly, calling the new nickname of one of the women and demanding a gift from her. The woman who has been called brings the candy or tobacco, and presents it to the drummer who asks for it. Then she dances while the men sing. Her movements are subdued and graceful, and she keeps both mukluks on the floor as she moves her body and her hands. The songs the men sing are unharmonized melodies based on a simple scale, and each song tells a little story. Some of the songs and dances are very old; others have been composed for the occasion.

When she has finished her dance, she joins the rest of the audience and another woman is summoned and gifts demanded. Not all the women dance—only those few who particularly enjoy it. Liz has always been shy about it, but toward the end of the evening some of her relatives call her out of the audience, and she dances with her eyes downcast.

After the dancing is over—it lasts for hours—the women carry out armloads of gifts that have been stashed in the other room and stack them around the hall. Then, starting with the oldest and continuing in order of age, the men pick out what they want from the mountain of gifts. Round and round they go, until the heap of gifts is gone. Charlie gets a new camp stove; his sons choose hunting equipment. Even little Evon scrambles away with a fistful of candy.

It's long after midnight when the first potlatch ends, but the next evening they start all over again. This time the women prepare the food for the men, and the women sing the songs and call the nicknames of the male dancers who perform sitting back on their heels, the leader of the group behind them. Their dances tell a story, and there is much joking and sly humor among them. This time the men give presents to the women, and when the dancing ends the gift-selecting begins, leading off with Mrs. Ivanoff. Liz picks bolts of fabric and a red fox fur; Anna carries off a heap of canned goods and some baby clothes; Louise acquires a leather purse and fancy socks; Mary gets a new *qaspeq*. It is early in the morning when the party finally ends.

Although this kind of social occasion is popular among the Yupik Eskimos, the potlatch has been associated primarily with the Indians of Southeastern and of western Canada. In the traditional Indian potlatch, now banned, one clan would invite another and heap lavish gifts on their guests, who were obligated to accept them and then to reciprocate later even more lavishly. This form of forced oneupmanship was sometimes used to reduce rival clans to poverty as well as to show off wealth and superiority. Oneupmanship is missing from the potlatches of Chaputnuak and other Eskimo villages, where the emphasis is on dancing and singing, the gifts are donated anonymously, and everybody gives as well as gets. Still, families often end up spending plenty of money for gifts to donate, a hardship when cash is short.

On Sunday morning after only a few hours of sleep the entire Koonuk family, Chaputnuak branch, attends mass, and the Moravian relatives prepare to return to Shnamute. Before they go, they invite the Koonuks to the rally that will be held in their church. Although Chaputnuak is a Catholic village, probably two-thirds of the people will make the trip south for a two-day song fest. Since no dancing is permitted in the Moravian church and

Eskimo singing is also taboo, the music will be strictly Protestant hymns. The main point in going, of course, is the chance it provides to visit friends and relatives. In a couple of weeks the Koonuks will head south again, following the trail of crossed sticks over the tundra. Eskimo rules of etiquette say that visitors may sleep or eat whereever they wish without prior invitation, returning the hospitality when visitors come to their village. And nobody ever knocks before entering.

Between these high points of social activity, the winter passes uneventfully. The mail planes come and go on an erratic schedule dictated by the weather. People worry sometimes about whether or not the fuel will hold out. Supplies of frozen, smoked, and preserved food gradually dwindle, but Egoak does a brisk business in canned goods. Except in the most extreme weather, the children play outdoors, sliding on the snowdrifts and playing a version of baseball on the frozen pond. Everybody misses the high school students in Bethel. Once in a while somebody flies in on business or for a look around. The name-exchange gifts are given, the hinted-for item packed in a box of useful items. The women work on their baskets. The men tinker with their snow machines and begin to think about seal hunting. The wheel of the year turns slowly toward spring.

February

THE OLD WOMAN IN A BIRDSKIN PARKA SITS IN A CIRCLE OF a dozen students and tells them what Bethel used to be like. The woman, Carrie Oscar, has lived all her life in this village that has grown into a city, and she likes to come to class once in a while and tell them how it was. While Carrie talks, Jim takes her picture for the school magazine, and Ilena translates what Carrie says into English for the Bethel Eskimos in the class who have not grown up speaking Yupik.

Carrie remembers when as many as six families shared one sod house, when women went without breakfast until their husbands came back from hunting, when many babies died at birth, when children worked hard, when Beluga whales swam in the Kuskokwim. It was different then, much different.

When Carrie's own memories run out, she repeats the stories her parents used to tell about the first Moravian missionaries. They returned to Pennsylvania after their first visit, but a year later they were back on a ship chartered from San Francisco, carrying on deck a small boat to bring their supplies up from the mouth of the river. The U.S. government gave them land on which to build a school and a church. That's when they renamed the fish camp Bethel.

After Carrie leaves, promising to come back and show them how to make a seal-gut window for a sod house, their teacher tells them of the many changes that transformed a village of a few dozen souls into a sprawling city. Some of the changes came about naturally. Of the 640 acres originally granted to the Moravians, only eleven have not been claimed by the Kuskokwim River as it changed course each spring during the flood that inevitably follows breakup.

Gradually people from the villages in the surrounding area began to migrate to Bethel. The missionaries offered education; traders offered goods in exchange for furs. As a result the population doubled every ten years. It has now leveled off at close to three thousand, about 85 percent of them Eskimo, too high a concentration to live off the land by hunting and fishing as their ancestors did. And there are not enough jobs to go around.

Although Bethel is located in an isolated area without the natural resources that have attracted whites to other parts of Alaska, Bethel has become a center of commerce for the Yukon-Kuskokwim Delta, a transportation center for much of Arctic Alaska, and an important defense loca-

tion for North America. As a result, Bethel is now head-
quarters for dozens of government agencies, some of them
employing natives but most of them staffed by whites who
work for the Public Health Service, the Civil Aeronautics
Board, the Fish and Game Commission, the National
Guard, VISTA, OEO, BIA, and so on through the alphabet
soup of federal, state, and local agencies. Many of these
whites are here only temporarily, until they move on to
the next duty assignment; most of them are housed in
compounds on the edge of town that keep them isolated
from most of the Eskimos who live near the river. Bethel is
in practice a segregated community.

In 1967 Bethel received national attention when it
was described as the poorest city in the United States.
Many of its inhabitants dwelled in miserable shacks; the
crime rate was high; alcoholism was a major problem. Although conditions seemed disgraceful to many white Americans, Eskimos from the villages saw Bethel in a quite
different light: it was an exciting place to go. Their villages,
where the sale of liquor was illegal, seemed dull by com-
parison. The liquor store and bars of Bethel were the main
attractions. They made the most money and paid the most
taxes; in fact they were considered the major economic
support of the town, as well as the source of most of its
problems. Eskimos who flocked to Bethel for a good time
often drank too much, passed out on the street, and quickly
died of exposure. The rate of deaths by freezing was ap-
pallingly high.

But then things began to improve. Federal grant

*Brown's Slough flows
past rickety Bethel dwellings
and into the Kuskokwim.*

money established the Kuskokwim Community College, a library, a public television station and twice-monthly newspaper, *Tundra Drums,* which describes itself as "relatively independent" and largely volunteer. There are a couple of big supermarket–department stores in Bethel filled with tempting gussak food and goods, a movie house with a different film every other night, and the big new Kuskokwim Inn. Architecture runs from prefabricated public buildings to quonset huts painted in loud colors to tenement shacks and a few old frame buildings that heave and tilt a little more with each cycle of thaw and freeze. A fleet of taxis chauffeurs residents and visitors from one end to the other of the biggest town on the tundra. Roads stop at the edge of town, but in winter the taxis drive on the frozen river to deliver passengers to nearby villages. The city fathers have tried to establish facilities that make Bethel sound like any unremarkable American town, such as a park with a pond for swimming and skating. But there is a community steam bath that stamps it as unmistakably Eskimo. Perhaps most important, the city has voted itself dry.

Life in Bethel is not easy by anybody's standards. In December of 1975, a fire destroyed the town's power plant. Although the federal government came to the rescue and flew in portable generators, pipes froze and burst, ruining many homes and spreading raw sewage throughout the town which remained safely frozen until spring thaw turned it into a health hazard. Like the Eskimos, white residents rely on a sense of humor for psychological survival. Near the small, lone evergreen tree that seems to grow by mistake along the road out to the airport, a large sign announces, "You are now entering Bethel National Forest."

There is a steady flow of native visitors to the cultural heritage class at the high school. One day a woman from a distant village shows the class how she makes a raincoat from seal gut, a fast-disappearing art. She holds up a translucent strip several yards long. The intestines of a seal, she explains, scraped and washed in urine and rinsed until they were perfectly clean. (The class is not surprised; human urine has a variety of practical uses, including medicinal: to treat a bleeding cut or drunk to reduce a high fever; to ice sled runners, to quick-thaw a frozen mechanical part. It has the advantage of ready availability.) The cleaned intestines were blown up to dry and then cut open to form a long strip about four inches wide. The visitor shows them how the strips are sewn horizontally, using dental floss to whip the seams over a strand of wild grass that keeps the floss from pulling through. (Before dental floss, she explains, women used animal sinew.) Sewing together enough strips for a coat is a laborious process, but the finished coat is lighter and more comfortable and long-wearing than rubber raingear. Resembling a shriveled skin when it is dried out, the coat must be hung in a damp place to keep it pliable. The seal-gut raincoat is not yet quite so rare as Carrie Oscar's birdskin parka, but the number of people who know how to make them—or who want to bother—is diminishing.

Jim keeps his mind on the woman making the raincoat with difficulty. He wants to know about the old tools and the old hunting methods, not about women's work. But the next visitor captures his imagination, an elderly man who was once a reindeer herder. After the Russian traders had decimated most of the Eskimos' game, Sheldon Jackson, the missionary leader, had brought reindeer from Siberia and later imported Lapp herders to teach the Eskimos the proper ways of herding. Eventually this became an occupation and a way of life for some natives. The old herder hypnotizes the class with descriptions of the hardships he experienced.

Later the teacher points out that reindeer are not the only animals to be successfully transplanted to Alaska. In 1931 a few musk oxen were brought from Greenland. Today a herd of eight hundred roams Nunivak Island, and big game hunters from other parts of Alaska and the Lower Forty-Eight draw lots and pay enormous fees for the privilege of shooting some of the animals each fall in a controlled program of keeping the herd thinned out and strong. The class marvels at white men who will pay so much money—the non-resident game fee alone is $1000—to kill one of the big, slow-moving beasts and have its head stuffed and mounted.

In this class—it was Ilena's idea that he sign up for it—Jim is learning more about his culture than he had ever known. But for many Eskimo students who have grown up in Bethel, it's virtually *all* they know about their culture. They don't speak Yupik, they don't know how to live off the land—in short, they don't know how to live as Eskimos, because their parents have forgotten how. And yet they find that they don't really know how to fit into the white world either.

But the whole class, village Eskimos and Bethel children, are learning something else: not all of Eskimo life is past history. There is a dynamic political present and future, too, and awareness of it crashes upon Jim Koonuk like a thunderbolt. His political science teacher, Mr. Wilson, has been explaining the Land Claims Settlement Act, its effect on the natives, and its possible effect on the future, including Jim's.

When Alaska became a state in 1959, it was given the right to select 103 million acres of land owned by the United States government. As the state began to take title to land it wanted, a question arose that white Alaskans had never considered before: who really owns Alaska? In 1966 several small associations got together to form the Alaska Federation of Natives (AFN), representing some sixty thousand Alaskan natives—Eskimo, Indian, and Aleut—who were arguing that the land really belonged to them. They had been there from the beginning. The whites had come only two hundred or so years ago, and one group of whites—the Russians—had sold land that did not belong to them to another group of whites—the Americans—who had no right to buy it. The AFN began to send bills to Washington, claiming that some of the land was rightfully theirs.

It was just as obvious to whites that Alaska was theirs,

because they had developed it. In the years when wildlife seemed the most important natural resource of the vast open tundras and rugged mountains, nobody took the philosophical question of ownership seriously. But in July 1968 Atlantic Richfield announced the discovery of one of the richest petroleum deposits in the world in Prudhoe Bay on the Arctic Coast. Within months, equipment and supplies were being flown from Fairbanks and Anchorage to Prudhoe. The following February three major oil companies announced their plans to build a forty-eight-inch pipeline to run eight hundred miles from Prudhoe to Valdez (val-DEEZ) on the Gulf of Alaska.

With the discovery of oil, the once philosophical question of land rights became a hotly contested issue. Secretary of the Interior Stewart L. Udall, who administered much of the land in Alaska for the U.S. government, stopped the transfer of federal land to the state until the native claims could be settled. Over the next few years there were demands and counter offers. Maintaining that each family on the barren tundra needs about two hundred fifty square miles of land on which to live by hunting, fishing, trapping, and foraging, the AFN demanded at least sixty million acres; the State of Alaska offered ten million acres, keeping the right to decide *which* land and the right to all income from oil and other minerals on that land.

Finally, in 1971, after years of lobbying and wrangling, Congress passed the Alaska Native Land Claims Settlement Act, turning over to the natives title to forty million acres of land in areas not already claimed by the state or withdrawn by the federal government. Although many whites were opposed to "handouts" of taxpayers' money, the Act also gave the natives 465 million dollars in federal funds and 500 million dollars in mineral rights—nearly a billion dollars in capital wealth put in the hands of people still unfamiliar with the gussaks' cash economy. The final bill was a heavy forty-eight pages, difficult enough for the layman fluent in English to understand, but virtually incomprehensible to the villagers whom it affected, even after it had been translated into the local language.

For purposes of handling this new wealth, Alaska was divided into twelve regional native corporations, each with an elected board of directors. Each region is made up of village corporations, one for each village with at least twenty-five residents. Bethel belongs to the regional corporation called Calista (pronounced cha-LIS-ta and meaning "our thing"), which includes fifty-six villages, far more than any other region. In villages like Chaputnuak, explanation of the Act and what it means to the people as individuals required many long meetings.

It had to be explained that the money would not come all at once to them, but over a period of years. That each person is an equal member in the corporation with 100 shares which cannot be sold for twenty years. That the money will be invested—in building a hotel in Anchorage, for example—to make more money. That the shareholders will receive dividend checks based on the money that the corporation earns.

There is so much to grasp. The village owns the surface of the land around it, enough for subsistence living, but the regional corporation owns what's under the surface, the mineral rights. The village is entitled to its share of half the money the regional corporation receives, whether from investments or from development of the mineral resources. There are so many ways to use that money: loans for native businesses, food and fishing cooperatives, educational programs, airports. The list of possibilities is endless. But the old people of the village have waited a long time and may not have many more years to wait. To make sure they receive their fair share while they are still alive, at least ten percent of the income received by the regional corporation is divided up and paid out in cash to each shareholder every three months for the first five years.

When the dividend checks began to come in, everyone breathed a little easier. Maybe this was going to work out after all. The villagers still depend on subsistence hunting and fishing and other sources of income, but the money is a help in coping with the cash economy—snow machines, boats, fuel—that has become a part of their lives.

Meanwhile, once the land claims were settled, pipeline construction began, over the objections of conservationists who argued that it would destory the delicate ecological balance of the area. Workers from the Lower Forty-Eight began to pour into the corridor from Anchorage and Valdez north through Fairbanks all the way to Prudhoe Bay. Tales of wealth were told: a fork-lift driver, for instance, could earn a thousand dollars in a twelve-hour-day, seven-day week—and could spend it just as quickly in Fairbanks and Anchorage, where inflation was soaring to undreamed of heights. Men in villages like Chaputnuak put in applications for the high-paying jobs, but most of the jobs were going to skilled workers from the south who held the right union card. The local men returned to their usual cash employment of commercial fishing in the summer and trapping in the winter. If the pipeline brought a bonanza to Alaska, very little of it reached the natives.

Once in a while some gussaks arrive in the villages of western Alaska carrying geophysical equipment. Surveying the land, they explain. Looking for oil, the people suspect. Sometimes the villagers have noticed an iridescent slick on the waters of the soggy tundra in the summer, and there's talk about what to do when the gussaks come and want right-of-way through their lands for another pipeline. Some, thinking of the potential wealth, look forward to it. Others, knowing what will follow, feel the price is too high. Some try to ignore it; some try to plan for it. A few intend to cash in on it. All know that when it comes right down to it, it is probably out of their hands, no matter what the law says.

Mr. Wilson, Jim's political science teacher, is a gussak, but he's a sympathetic man, and the Eskimo students like him. A bearded, bushy-haired young man with wire-rimmed glasses, he lives down by the river in the native section, rather than in the school compound.

Some people say the Eskimo culture is dying, he tells the native students. In another generation nobody will grow up knowing how to speak Yupik; they'll all have to take courses to learn it in school. The crafts, the ancient dances, the old ways of hunting and fishing—they'll be like scenes in a museum. That's why it's so important not only to preserve the old ways by studying them, but to keep on living them. But in the meantime, it's just as important to learn white man's ways, in order to take advantage of the best of both worlds.

The hardest thing, Wilson tells them, is figuring out what *is* the best. Lots of gussaks aren't particularly happy with what their society is all about either—the pollution, the fast pace, lots of things. It's up to young Eskimos to understand what the laws are all about, and to use them for the natives' benefit—like investing the funds from the corporation wisely, so that needed cash will come into the village that way, rather than from welfare.

The villagers are getting smarter though, Wilson tells them, and tougher. There was a time when Eskimos considered it such bad manners to say "no" to a white man that they simply smiled and let all kinds of disastrous things happen. But now they're learning to speak up, to stand their ground. He reminds them of the time in 1975 when the Bureau of Land Management sent representatives from Anchorage to some of the larger villages for open hearings about "utility corridors" that the government wanted to establish. What the BLM was after was an *easement,* a legal term meaning that the government has the right to use privately owned land for certain stated purposes. Nothing was going to be built yet, but the easements meant that pipelines, roads, even canals could eventually be put right through the land the natives had just been given.

Most of the villages didn't know what the easements were all about, and only a few people attended the hearings. It was different in Bethel; seventy-four people showed up and told the BLM representatives quite plainly how they felt, in front of microphones and television cameras that broadcast their testimony to all the villages in the area. They described how such construction threatened the balance of life in the tundra and ultimately affected their own survival. Firmly, they said NO to the white men. The outcome is still open at the time this is being written, but the Alaska Federation of Natives has urged "proper study" for all proposed corridors and insisted that no corridors should be planned through lands given to the Eskimos by the Native Land Claims Settlement Act.

At about the same time; sports hunters and other special interest groups, afraid that natives would put up "No Trespassing" signs around their land, began to pressure the Secretary of the Interior to use his authority to establish "recreational easements" along the coast, through the rivers, and around the lakes. When this latest invasion began against their newly won property, much of it still not yet theirs in writing, thirty-four villages in Calista asked their corporation to go to court and fight the federal government, the greatest of all "Indian givers."

"This is the kind of thing your people face all the time," Wilson tells his students. "What the Eskimos need now are strong young leaders who can meet the white man on his own terms. Teachers, too. I'm about to become obsolete, if I'm not already, and so are all the white teachers around here. How many Eskimo teachers are there here in

Bethel? Sometimes two or three, and the rest are white. But that's changing. About time, too."

Wilson launches into a brief rundown of education in the area. First came the missionaries with their schools. Then in 1913 the federal government built a school in Bethel. In 1931 the government agency that was eventually named the Bureau of Indian Affairs took over responsibility for education of Alaskan natives. Over a period of years the BIA set up thirty-two schools in the Yukon-Kuskokwim area.

When Alaska became a state it accepted, at least in principle, responsibility for running the schools for natives as well as whites. But since the state wasn't ready to take over the job entirely, the shift was gradual. For a few years, villages had a choice of state, BIA, or local education programs, an option that created even more problems in educating a few people spread out over a huge area.

Then came another change. In 1975 the state legislature disbanded the Alaska State Operated School System and set up in its place Regional Education Attendance Areas to be run by local school boards. In February 1976, Region 4, which includes Bethel, elected a nine-member board to take over the following July. Not only did the inexperienced board members have to oversee the change from state to local control, but they also had a budget of $4.5 million dollars and fourteen hundred students to worry about. On top of that, the board has a deadline of September 1, 1977, for establishing a high school program in any village that asks for one, either by building a new school, using the existing elementary school for double shifts, or setting up correspondence courses. Even with that big budget, one of the worst problems is money. Nearly half the cost of operating a modern school on the tundra goes just for electricity. That cost used to be paid for by the BIA out of a separate budget; now it will have to come out of money that ought to be spent on education.

The bell rings and the social studies class ends. His head spinning with political problems, Jim collects his books and starts for the door. Mr. Wilson stops him with a hand on his shoulder. "What about you?" he asks. "Have you thought about going on to college? You could be a lot of help to your people. There's scholarship money available. And you've certainly got the brains, if you wouldn't spend so much time thinking about seal hunting."

Jim keeps his eyes on the floor, embarrassed that Mr. Wilson knows what he is thinking. But there's more to it than seal hunting. His parents want him to get an education, to be able to make money. They also want him to come home to the village when he graduates from high school. They are afraid that with a college education—in addition to meaning four more years away from home—he will have no desire to come back to live in the village again. And that, finally, is what most parents want for their children, more than an education—more, even, than good jobs.

What does Jim want for himself? He wishes he knew.

March

GIGGLING AT THE ANTICS OF *Sesame Street's* BIG BIRD ON television, Louise doesn't notice the dropped stitch until she has knitted two rows past it. "Uminukfa!" she mutters —"Darn it"—and begins to unravel the woolen cap she is knitting for her boyfriend, Larry. This is the second time she has had to rip out her stitches. It annoys her—but not enough to turn off the television. She wants to finish the cap soon, a surprise for Larry, in time for seal hunting. Larry Egoak graduated from high school in Bethel three years ago. His father, Ted Egoak, who owns the village store, wanted him to go to college, but Larry is not a particularly ambitious young man. He decided he would rather stay in Chaputnuak and help out in the store.

Louise is not the only girl in the village who is interested in Larry: in fact, he only recently broke up with one of her friends. About a month ago Louise went to the store to buy sugar for her mother, and she and Larry started talking. He offered her a can of orange soda, and they talked some more. Louise did not get back with the sugar for over an hour. After that Louise found a reason to go to the store almost every day. Then she began to meet him again in the evening. Larry's father had given him a powerful snowmobile for Christmas, and they went for rides out on the river. Louise straddled the seat behind him and hung on tight while he opened the throttle and the machine roared over the hard snow.

Two weeks ago they went to the store after the Friday night movie—"For sodas," Larry said. Larry didn't switch on the lights in the store, but he did turn the stove up higher. They settled down on a pile of blankets in the corner and began to kiss. Then Larry slid his hands inside her parka. Louise was frightened and insisted that she had to go home. But a few days later Larry asked her to go back to the store with him, and she went, although she knew what would probably happen. She told herself that it would not go any further, and for two more visits to the store she was able to keep it that way. She certainly did not want to end up in her sister Anna's situation! But the kissing got more and more passionate, and the last time they went to the store Louise was not able to stop Larry or to stop herself.

Since then she has felt miserable. She is no longer a virgin, and she believes that she has committed a sin. But she is also afraid she might have gotten pregnant. If they do it again—and Louise is afraid they will and at the same time afraid they won't if she didn't please him enough—she will ask him to do something to protect her. Until Louise started going with Larry, her relationships with boys had been rather naive. Once in a while she had hung around outside the community center, sipping cans of soda after the Saturday night movie. And once in a while she had gone for walks with one of the boys she liked, holding hands and sometimes kissing. When she learned about sex at school, it seemed like something far away that had nothing to do with her. Houses are small, privacy is minimal, and children grow up with an awareness of sex that takes away much of the mysteriousness. The church preaches its moral values of abstinence before marriage and fidelity in marriage, but the parents say little. Louise wishes she could talk to somebody about this, but she doesn't know to whom. Not her mother, certainly. Not her friends . . . did Larry do this with her friend Agnes, too? If only she could talk to Anna . . .

Sex isn't Louise's only problem. Once when they went to the store, to the pile of warm blankets, Larry offered her a cigarette. She shook her head; she doesn't smoke. But this was not a regular cigarette, he explained. It was marijuana. A friend had brought it from Bethel. It was easy to get there; everyone smoked pot in Bethel, he claimed. Larry showed Louise how to inhale it, hold it in her lungs, and let it out slowly. When she didn't do it right, he got annoyed with her and finished the joint himself. It seemed to put him in a good mood, and at least he doesn't drink.

With a high school diploma
an Eskimo girl
faces the future.

Louise wonders who else in the village smokes marijuana. Does her brother Jim? It's impossible to ask him, but it seems important to know.

Louise has just gotten her knitting repaired when the dog barks to announce the arrival of Carl and Anna. Carl carries Christine, and Anna lags behind them, walking slowly, the front of her parka bulging. They tell Liz that they have decided it's time for Anna to leave for Bethel. The baby is due in about three weeks, but it's better to go too soon rather than wait too long.

Anna will stay at the pre-maternal home in Bethel until labor begins. She dreads this lonely wait, without Carl or Christine or her mother to keep her cheered up. Deciding when to leave the village depends partly on the time of year and weather conditions. If she waits too long, she might get caught in an early breakup and not be able to leave the village. None of the women want to have their babies at home any more—it's safer to go to the hospital— although until recent years few made the trip.

Christine, set down on the floor, so bundled up she can scarcely waddle, nevertheless makes her way straight to Louise, who picks her up and kisses her and begins to peel off her boots and heavy parka. Anna asks her mother if she will take care of Christine until after the new baby is born, and Liz readily agrees.

Charlie and Liz were not particularly happy about Anna's marriage to Carl. He came from another village, where he had a reputation as a hell-raiser. Then he and Anna met at a church rally, and the two young people were immediately attracted to each other. Anna was nineteen and quietly pretty; Carl was tall for an Eskimo and a member of the National Guard. They began to see a lot of each other. When Anna discovered that she was pregnant, there was no thought of an abortion. Carl seemed pleased that there was to be a child, and they had immediately decided to marry. Although Liz and Charlie were not as impressed with Carl as Anna appeared to be, it was her choice and they would never interfere with her decision of whom to marry, no matter how they felt.

Before missionaries came to the villages, marriage was a simple matter. When a young Eskimo was a proven hunter and ready to take on the responsibilities of wife and family, his parents picked out a young girl to be his wife, talked it over with her parents, and if they agreed, the young man simply moved in with the girl and her parents. If she accepted him, the matter was settled. They lived with her parents until they had children and established a home of their own. If it didn't seem satisfactory—if the wife was not a good worker, or if she did not produce children—the husband left. Anna's mother told her old Mrs. Ivanoff was married for the first time when she was only thirteen, and she has been married several times since then.

But when the priests came, all that changed. The church does not approve of arranged marriages, and Father William makes sure the couple has known each other for several months before he lets them get married. As Anna saw the situation, the priests make you get married in church, and then they make you stay with the person you

married. They don't say you have to get along with that
person, though, and everybody could name a few couples
who don't get along at all.

Before Anna's wedding took place, one of the older
women of the village, a cousin of Liz's, invited Anna for a
visit. While the two sipped tea, the woman lectured Anna
on the responsibilities of marriage. It was not something to
be taken lightly; she must understand well her role as a
helper to her husband and as a mother to their children.
Anna listened silently, eyes lowered. This form of pre-
marital counseling is traditional in the village. She knew
that one of the older men had taken Carl aside for the same
purpose, to emphasize the importance of the step they were
about to take, to caution him to care for and protect his
wife and children.

The wedding had been simple enough. Everyone was
invited to the church late one afternoon. Anna and her
parents and other relatives entered without fanfare and sat
near the front. Anna wore slacks and new tennis shoes and
the handsome zipper jacket that Carl had given her. Carl,
resplendent in his National Guard uniform, came in later
with his friends and sat in back with them. When Father
William arrived, the bridal couple and their witnesses
walked uncertainly to the altar, and the Roman Catholic
ceremony began in English. Someone took Polaroid snap-
shots during the ceremony; the pictures showed a somber
bride and groom. Afterwards Anna's parents gave a dinner
at the community center, and when the food had been
cleared away, Charlie Koonuk entertained his guests with

a special showing of a western movie.

Then everyone went home. Carl accompanied Anna to her parents' house, but he didn't stay long. Anna slept on her cot alone, as usual, and the bridegroom went out to celebrate with his friends. Charlie found him the next morning, very drunk, asleep on the porch of the community center. Two weeks after the wedding Carl left for the cannery in Dillingham, and Anna stayed with her parents. When he came back, they arranged to buy an old house that no one had lived in for years. It was a poor place, Charlie said; it would have made a better fish house. But Anna wanted a home of her own, and it was all they could afford.

Alone in their own home, they did not have sex together. Anna was hurt and puzzled. Carl said it was because she was pregnant, and he didn't want to hurt the baby. Later she found out it was because he had a venereal disease. Although he was cured of it rather quickly, Anna worries now. She knows that he probably sleeps with other women when he is away from home, if not with one of the girls at the cannery, then with prostitutes in Anchorage when he goes there for National Guard training. Anna understands that this is the way of men, and she tries not to think about it.

Early missionaries had a lot of convincing to do when they first reached the Eskimos, whom they regarded as pagans entirely without morals. Although the bond between husband and wife was strong, it did not necessarily imply sexual exclusivity. In the old days, wife-lending was a common practice, a courtesy extended to friends and visitors just as one offered food and lodging. It was the husband's decision, however, and a wife's refusal to be part of her husband's hospitality—or to offer it without his approval—could lead to serious trouble. Courtesy was not the only reason for wife-lending: the inability of one partner to produce children could be disastrous in a society where children are highly valued. Exchanging partners improved the odds. The missionaries became accustomed to many Eskimo practices, but not that one. And so the Christianized Eskimos gradually accepted the sexual mores imposed on them by the white man, as well as the hypocrisy that is part of those mores. There is no more custom of wife-lending, but there is some "playing around," both before and during marriage.

When the time has come for Anna to leave for Bethel, the pilot boosts her up the high step and into the front seat of the airplane. Carl waves to her, but there is no embrace, no kiss, no public show of affection from either of them. Once in Bethel her anxiety and depression begin to lift when she discovers that an acquaintance from Shnamute is also waiting at the pre-maternal home. While they wait for their babies, the two settle down to chat and drink tea and work on baskets and beads for the home to sell. Time seems to drag by, but on the tenth day of the wait Carl arrives for a surprise visit. At first Anna is pleased—until she realizes that he has been drinking. Then she suspects that the trip was mainly to get a bottle of bootleg liquor, and she is upset that he has spent so much money: plane fare plus vodka have cost nearly a hundred dollars. When she mentions it to him, he flies into a rage and storms out of the home. That night labor begins, and Anna is taken to the hospital in the van that always stands ready for this trip. Before she leaves, she asks her friend to call around Bethel and see if she can locate Carl before he goes back home. "Tell him his son is being born!"

Hours later in the hospital delivery room, the doctor shows Anna her new baby, a fine healthy girl with a thick black head of hair. Anna smiles and reaches out for her new daughter, but she is already thinking what Carl will say and do.

Carl says nothing. He is too drunk to talk. The nurse who finally located him in Lousetown, the poorest section of Bethel, made the mistake of telling him he had a daughter, and Carl has consumed most of a quart of vodka. Anna is philosophical. Whether disappointed over a girl or elated over a boy, he *still* would have gotten drunk. But he is sober again when it is time to take Anna and the new baby back to Chaputnuak a few days later. They have decided to name her Sally, but Carl has also said he wants Liz and Charlie to adopt her.

Although the family is happy about the new baby, there is a great sadness in their hearts. Old Frances Koonuk, Charlie's mother, is very sick. She had seemed for some time to be moving more slowly, to be getting tired much faster. She had not spent so much time out on the tundra last summer, gathering eggs and grasses and picking berries. When cold weather came, she hardly left the house—not even to go ice fishing, which she had always loved. She used to pride herself on her strength, but lately it seemed to be leaking away.

A few days after Anna and Sally fly home from the hospital, Nathaniel Koonuk hurries to the clinic and asks Marie to come and see his wife. She finds the old lady lying motionless in the bed under a pile of quilts. After taking her temperature and blood pressure and pulse and asking a few questions, Marie returns to the clinic and radios the hospital in Bethel. The doctor there decides on the basis of Marie's report that it would be best to have Frances come in as soon as possible. He will authorize this as an emergency flight, and Frances will not have to pay.

When Marie goes back to the old people's house, she finds Nathaniel pacing the floor and a half-dozen relatives silently drinking tea. Marie reports the doctor's decision and offers to stop by the home of the man who is the agent for one of the airlines that serves the villages. Minutes later she comes back to report that a plane is on its way to Shnamute with a passenger and some freight, and it will stop at Chaputnuak on the return trip.

Nathaniel looks even more worried and upset. Would it be possible for him to go with his wife to the hospital? Marie says there will probably be space on the plane, but he must understand that the hospital will not pay his fare. Charlie tells him not to worry; they will pay his way. Nathaniel agrees. He cannot let his wife go alone. She is afraid, he explains. He does not need to explain that he, too, is afraid.

The family helps get the old couple ready for the trip. Then they sit and wait, talking little, now and then checking the shabby suitcase. Frances does not speak or change expression. Finally the word comes that the plane has left Shnamute; it will arrive in fifteen minutes.

They dress the grandmother warmly, tie her mukluks around her swollen ankles, wrap her carefully in a blanket. David Koonuk hooks the wooden sled to the back of his snow machine. His father gets in first. Then Charlie and David carry their mother out of the house and lay her in the sled next to their father, who holds her as though she were a big doll. Slowly and carefully, choosing the route with the smoothest trail, David drives his parents out to the airstrip. Charlie follows with Liz and his sister-in-law. When the plane lands, they lift Frances from the sled and slide her into the seat and fasten the seat belt around her. Nathaniel crawls in next to her. By the time they are ready to leave, Andy and Mary and Louise have gathered around the plane. Then the plane takes off and the children, quite subdued, pile into Charlie's sled for the ride back home.

A week later, the family is notified by the hospital that Frances is dead. Mr. Frederickson, director of the student dorm in Bethel, takes Jim and Pete to his office and gently breaks the news to them. Excused from classes, the boys get ready to fly home with the grandfather and their grandmother's body for the funeral and burial.

Nathaniel Koonuk's deeply lined face is streaked with tears. The boys solemnly shake hands with him. No one speaks during the hour-long flight, and a silent gathering of family and friends meets them at the village airstrip. The body, in a plain plywood coffin, is placed on the sled of a snowmobile and pulled slowly home over the ice. The body has not been embalmed, but Frances's daughters perform the task of washing it and dressing it in her best parka. Some of her belongings are put into the coffin with her: the *ulu* with which she had butchered so many seals, an unfinished beadwork necklace, an ivory crucifix. One of the daughters gathers up the rest of her possessions; they will be burned after the funeral. Nothing material is passed on to others.

Before the arrival of Christian missionaries, the Eskimos did not bury their dead but put them in small driftwood houses built on top of the ground. On the outside of the little house they hung the personal belongings of the dead person—kitchenware, hunting tools, combs, jewelry. But on the day of Frances's funeral, half a dozen men of the village take turns digging down through several feet of snow into the frozen earth. The digging is a struggle, and they manage to excavate only a shallow grave. In the summer when the snow is gone and the tundra is spongey, they will dig it deeper. Then some of the older couples will get together and spend a day fixing up the cemetery, straightening and painting the white crosses, mending the fence, arranging plastic flowers on the graves.

That afternoon the men carry the coffin to the church

where the mourners have gathered. Nearly everyone in town is present, for Frances Koonuk was much liked in the village. Andy is the only member of the family who does not sit with the others; newly confirmed, he is assisting Father William at the mass for the dead. While the priest's voice drones on, Charlie Koonuk tries to restrain Evon, who wriggles and squirms and talks aloud, occasionally breaking loose to run back the aisle of the crowded church to find someone else he knows. Liz sits with her arm around Mary, who leans close to her. Next to them Anna nurses Sally and wonders if Carl really meant it when he told her to ask her parents to take the baby. Christine, face smeared with candy, snuggles contentedly on Carl's lap and sucks the lollipop he gave her.

Louise watches her sister with the infant Sally and worries what to do if she is really pregnant as she fears she may be. Larry is not at the funeral; he is not even in Chaputnuak. He left for Bethel, on business for his father, and he did not even tell her he was going. Mr. Egoak explained when she went to look for Larry at the store, but she was too shy and embarrassed to ask when he would be back.

Pete sits behind his father, his mind on seal hunting. Last night when he arrived for the funeral, his uncle Wally took him aside and asked him if he wanted to go with them this year. They would soon be taking the boats down to the sea. Pete, full of excitement, has decided that he will not go back to school with Jim tomorrow. He plans to tell his family tonight that he would rather stay here and go hunting. Pete wants Jim to stay, too, but Jim has already said that he will not.

Jim's mind is on a hundred things all at once: on Ilena and her ambitions, on his teacher who thinks he should go to college, on his parents and what they want him to do. Everybody seems to have something different in mind for him. But gradually he has gotten an idea of his own: maybe he could learn some practical skill, like building construction. With talk of the new schools that might be put up in some of the villages, with all the projects the regional corporation has in mind, he would have lots of chances to use that skill. He could even build his parents a nice home, and one for himself someday, right here in the village. There would be plenty of chance for hunting and fishing, and enough money to go on trips—to Anchorage and Hawaii on vacations. He could have the best of both worlds: a traditional life with a good income. He's anxious to ask Ilena what she thinks of the idea. Jim Koonuk watches the tears flow unashamedly down his grandfather's careworn face, listens to the drone of the priest, and dares to dream of his own future.

Epilogue

THE MORNING JET FROM ANCHORAGE SKIDDED INTO BETHEL
airport in a freezing rain, carrying a heavy load of freight
and an assortment of passengers. Most of them were whites
with government or private business in Bethel or in one of
the villages. A few were Eskimos, like the mother and her
children returning from a visit to relatives in the city.

Also on board was Carolyn Meyer, the author of this
book, bleary-eyed from a long flight from New York and
a five-hour time difference. Out of the crowd in the bus-
tling log-cabin terminal stepped Bernadine Larsen. Although we had never met, we recognized each other
immediately. We had been corresponding for a long time,
and from our friendship by mail we had decided to work
on a book together about a mutually fascinating subject:
Eskimo family life.

We bring to the project entirely different backgrounds. Larsen was for thirteen years a Roman Catholic nun, a member of the Order of Notre Dame. In 1969 as Sister Margaretta Burke, she realized her dream of working in Alaska. Through a Jesuit volunteer program she went to the village of Chefornak to establish a preschool program. While Sister Marge was in Chefornak, she decided to leave the order. She did so, later returning to the village to work as a lay volunteer. In 1973 she married an Eskimo, Jimmie Larsen, and started a family. The villagers still call her Marge, and except for the priest and the BIA teachers, she is the only gussak in town.

Meanwhile, Carolyn Meyer was living in Norwalk, Connecticut, writing children's books and teaching a correspondence course for people who wished to learn to write for children. One of the students assigned to her was Bernadine Larsen. We developed both a professional and a personal relationship. Out of it evolved the idea of writing this book.

Meyer had the advantage of metropolitan libraries and research facilities. Larsen's advantage is obvious: she's there. After months of exchanging tapes and research notes, a visit was arranged. On March 1, 1976, Meyer and Larsen finally got together.

During the visit Larsen fed her guest raw whitefish, smoked salmon dipped in seal oil, and *akutaq*. Meyer prepared her own native dish, Pennsylvania Dutch chicken potpie, for her hosts. Meyer, having read about the Eskimo penchant for tea, brought a gift of a handmade teapot and a carton of assorted blends. Larsen countered with a gift of mukluks made by her mother-in-law. But mostly the two talked and listened—to each other and to people in Chefornak and other villages.

They created a fictional village and peopled it with fictional characters. They named their village Chaputnuak, for an extinct village that once stood on the site now occupied by Chefornak. Chaputnuak, meaning "place where the rocks stick out," is not meant to be exactly like Chefornak, but rather like many similar Eskimo villages in the Yukon-Kuskokwim Delta. And the Koonuks are not like any particular family; rather, a composite of many different people. The situations and problems, though, are real enough.

Later that same month, Meyer took her suitcase full of notes and souvenirs and made the long trip home again. Along the way, John McDonald, photographer for *Tundra Drums,* was recruited to supply photographs. In the months that followed, rough drafts of each chapter were mailed from Norwalk to Chefornak and back again with corrections and comments. McDonald sent pictures. Meyer moved to Pennsylvania. Larsen got pregnant with her third child.

Finally the book was finished.

December 1976